THE DIARY O

JACK THE RI

 25 YEARS OF MYSTERY 

RESEARCH & CONCLUSION

SHIRLEY HARRISON, JAMES JOHNSTON,
KIERAN JAMES, RICHARD C. COBB,
KEITH SKINNER, PAUL BUTLER,
ROBERT ANDERSON & PROF. DAVID CANTER

First published and printed by Secret Chamber Publishing,
Whitechapel, London. September 2017

ISBN 978-1-9998538-0-8

ACKNOWLEDGEMENTS

The authors of The Diary of Jack the Ripper: Research and Conclusion would like to acknowledge and thank, in no particular order, those who have helped to bring this book to life.

How Brown
Rob Clack
Daisy O'Quigley
Lauren Davies
Colin B Leonard
Mick Priestley
Katja Nieder
Rebecca Cobb
Johanne Edgington
Alessandro Mana
Dave Stokes
Amy Harper
Mark Ripper
Phil Carter
Elizabeth Quinn
Paul Begg
Livia Triviata
Robert Smith
John Chambers
James Dickey
Colin Cobb
Steve Jessop
Richard Patterson
Jamie Biddle
Lindsay Siviter
Bruce Robinson
Caroline Morris
Rob Clack

THE DIARY OF JACK THE RIPPER: RESEARCH AND CONCLUSION

CONTENTS

Tempus Omnia Revelat

TEMPUS OMNIA REVELAT

INTRODUCTION

25 YEARS LATER

BY SHIRLEY HARRISON
AUTHOR OF THE DIARY OF JACK THE RIPPER

1993, seems a lifetime ago, but that was the year in which I took a call from my literary agent, Doreen Montgomery, inviting me to her office in London. She had received a call from a Michael Barrett in Liverpool who claimed to have found the diary of Jack the Ripper and wanted to bring it to show her.

That meeting was to launch me overnight into a world about which none of us had absolutely any previous knowledge, peopled with scientists, historians and international experts in criminology. My own previous books had included a history of the English Channel, an investigation into the world of religious cults and a biography of Father Christmas. This was very unfamiliar ground.

Mike Barrett told us how he had acquired the book from a mate in Liverpool who had recently died and now he wanted to get it published. The diary itself was about 1" thick with a hard cover. Each page was filled with the demented outpourings of a madman. The writing veered wildly from neat, to the sprawling blood-thirsty confessions of a callous killer, whose murderous rampage in Whitechapel in 1888 became an international horror story.

It was signed *"Yours truly Jack the Ripper."*

There was no mention anywhere of "Jack the Ripper's" real identity. The only clue was a statement on page two of the diary – *"tonight I shall return to Battlecrease".* What was Battlecrease and where was it?

Neither Doreen nor I had ever been confronted by such a challenge. It was to overtake my life for the next 25 years!

The first step of course was to find a publisher willing to gamble on a very uncertain project. That publisher proved to be Robert Smith, then of Smith Gryphon and I found myself – a novice - launched into the world of experts in criminology, handwriting, ink, and, of course legions of international and mostly hostile Ripper historians. At the time, I had absolutely no idea how passionate was the world I was about to enter. I was faced with deep skepticism from many. But there were a few who, like me, were fascinated - especially once ink and handwriting tests eventually proved that the book had, at least, been written in the late 19th century and was definitely not a modern forgery.

So, it was that I set out with my friend and co researcher, Sally Evemy, on our first of many visits to Liverpool where we had meetings with the bewildered descendants of some of the people referred to in the book, by then known to us as "The Diary of Jack the Ripper."

The quest eventually led us to identify its author as a Liverpool cotton merchant - James Maybrick, who, in the late 19th century lived, with his young wife Florence, in a splendid mansion overlooking the cricket field. Its name? *"Battlecrease"*!

James Maybrick was a drug-taking socialite on the Liverpool scene. His wealthy and highly connected brother, Michael, lived in London and James made frequent visits to meet him in the capital. James' own office was on the edge of Whitechapel where he also had a house - and a mistress. Not the most obvious candidate to be Jack the Ripper!

When James Maybrick died in 1889, his young wife, Florence, was unjustifiably accused of his murder by poison and sentenced to life imprisonment. She had been having an affair herself with a Liverpool cotton broker named Alfred Brierley - who immediately emigrated to America before the trial and only returned many years later, to live in the little Sussex village of Newick where he is buried.

The Maybrick story and trial was well known and in the following years many books have been written and films made and for the first time, the name of Maybrick was linked with that of Jack the Ripper. It was all the stuff of which a writer's dreams are made.

The research that followed took Sally and me to all corners of the British Isles to speak to descendants of anyone who knew or were related to the Maybricks. We went to the Isle of Wight, to Wales and Scotland .

A phone call from the delightful Albert Johnson in Liverpool ,resulted in a meeting with him at our publisher's office to look at a watch, which he had recently bought for his grand-daughter. Inside, and barely legible, were the scratched words *"J.Maybrick I am Jack"*!!!

From then on, we found ourselves in the unfamiliar world of experts in history, ink, and handwriting. We explored among many other, sometimes intimidating, sources such as the London Patent Office, Somerset House, the American State archives, the College of Heralds, the British Medical Association and Scotland Yard.

On publication - the controversy exploded worldwide and I was invited to appear, also on radio and television, in America, Canada, France and Germany. The Diary even was translated into Japanese. A fellow writer, the late Stanley Dangar, flew in from Spain and Sally and I discovered a number of rather puzzled descendants of James Maybrick in various parts of Britain. Exploratory, but inconclusive, documentary films were made which only added fuel to the fire and the debate rages on today.

Since then my writing has taken a very different course....into the worlds, among others, of Winnie-the-Pooh and Sylvia Pankhurst.

But the controversy around the Maybrick Diary continued and continues, unabated and undemolished. Today there are even Jack the Ripper tours for tourists - and now a Conference – in Liverpool. Maybe the epitaphs on the graves of three of the key players in the drama are there to tell us something?

Michael Maybrick moved to the Isle of Wight, where he became Mayor and a hugely respected dignitary. He was given the equivalent of a state funeral.

The message on his rather splendid tomb is *"There shall be no more death."*

Alfred Brierley died in Newick. His gravestone message is *"And a Sewer went Forth."*

And James himself? The message on the Coat of Arms which he bought from the College of Arms before his marriage in 1881 reads ominously *"Tempus Omnia Revelat"* – *"Time reveals All"*! ...or Does It?

CHAPTER 1

THE MAYBRICK FAMILY

BY JAMES JOHNSON

James Maybrick

Born:	24nd October 1838, Liverpool
Parents:	William Maybrick, Susannah Wainwright
Spouse:	Florence Maybrick
Children:	James 'Bobo' Maybrick, Gladys Evelyn Maybrick
Death:	11th May 1889, Liverpool

James Maybrick was born in Liverpool, to parents William and Susannah, on 24th October 1838. James was the third of seven children – two of which, did not survive into adulthood. Little is known about Maybrick's upbringing, or the larger influences that bore upon his future. In his early twenties, James left the family home and travelled to London, working in a ship brokering office. It was there that he met Sarah Ann Robertson; his first lover. Sarah would remain Maybrick's mistress for the best part of twenty years. In 1874, at the age of thirty-six, James travelled to Norfolk, Virginia, where he started the American end of his transatlantic cotton business. Whilst there, Maybrick contracted malaria and was given a prescription of arsenic and strychnine, 'medicines' which he would remain addicted to until death.

In March 1880, during one of his trans-Atlantic crossings, James met Florence Elizabeth Chandler; an eighteen-year old, Southern American belle from Mobile, Alabama. Over the course of the six-day voyage, the pair sparked a 'lightning romance' and resolved to be married on 21st July 1881, at St. James' Church, Piccadilly. Following the birth of their son Bobo, on 24th March 1882, the family relocated to Liverpool; renting a detached house in the exclusive sub-burb of Grassendale. Their daughter, Gladys Evelyn was born 20th July 1886.

Throughout his time in Liverpool, James Maybrick was an active freemason. The earliest known reference to him having taken the Masonic oath is dated 31st December 1869. Like the rest of the city's elite, James was a member of at least three lodges; the St. George's Lodge of Harmony (35), the Liverpool Chapter (19) and the Royal Arch Chapter, Jerusalem (32). Outside of Liverpool, James was also a member of the Orpheus Lodge (1706), which was one of his brother Michael's more prominent London lodges.

In February 1888, the Maybricks moved into Battlecrease House; taking up a five-year lease on the property. Their marriage, however, was crumbling. Florence, who had learned of Maybrick's mistress, had kindled a relationship with Alfred Brierley; a cotton broker and business acquaintance of James'. As far as the official record is concerned, their marital turmoil culminated in March 1889, when Florence visited London soliciting firm Markby, Stewart & Company, seeking a divorce from her husband.

The spring of 1889 would be Maybrick's last; his health finally succumbing to the ravages of long-term drug abuse. He died in the arms of his best friend, George Davidson, on 11th May 1889. Brothers Edwin and Michael, suspicious as to the cause of death, had his body examined. It was found to contain slight traces of arsenic, but not enough to be considered fatal. The cause of death, as recorded on his death certificate, was recorded; 'Irritant poison, administered to him by Florence Maybrick. Wilful murder.' Florence was duly arrested and tried for James' murder, a charge to which she was found guilty and sentenced to death. After much public outcry, the sentence was commuted to life imprisonment, of which she would serve fifteen years before release in 1904. The exact circumstances of James' death have remained an issue of debate amongst researchers. As knowledge and understanding of the case has developed, suspicion has accumulated around brothers Edwin and Michael.

The Maybricks & their children at home

Chapter 1

Florence Elizabeth Maybrick

MRS. MAYBRICK.
Copyright photo by Medrington, Liverpool.

Born:	3rd September 1862, Mobile, Alabama
Parents:	William George Chandler, Caroline Holbrook
Spouse:	James Maybrick
Children:	James 'Bobo' Maybrick, Gladys Evelyn Maybrick
Death:	23rd October 1941, South Kent, Connecticut

Florence Elizabeth Maybrick was born on 3rd September 1862, to parents William George Chandler and Caroline Chandler Du Barry, in the prosperous sea-port of Mobile, Alabama. Florie's mother, Caroline Holbrook, was from a socially elevated New York family, whilst her father William was an eminent Southern banker. Florie's father died when she was still a child. The family spent the following years travelling between New York and the European cities of Paris, Cologne and St. Petersburg. Consequently, Florence and her only brother, Holbrook, received interrupted educations.

In March 1880, Florence and her mother boarded the SS Baltic, a luxurious steamer bound from New York to Liverpool. James Maybrick was also on board ship. Despite the disparity in both age and upbringing, Florence and James experienced something of a 'lightning romance'. Sixteen months later, they married at St. James' Church, Piccadilly. Later, some would wonder whether Florence had set out to ensnare James, asking whether her feelings had been genuine. Nevertheless, Florence would bear James two children; James (Bobo) Maybrick born in March 1884, and Gladys Evelyn Maybrick, born in July 1886. By the time Gladys arrived, Florence and James were struggling to conceal their escalating difficulties.

In December 1887, Florence discovered that James had been keeping a long-term mistress; Sarah Ann Robertson. According to author Kate Colquhoun; 'She never said how she knew – perhaps she came across bills or accounts that gave the game away – but the sure knowledge of her husband's calculated, long-term infidelity dealt a final, shattering blow.' (Colquhoun, 2014). Soon, rumours began to circulate as to the nature of Florence's relationship with James' colleagues, including his brother Edward. One man, an attractive, thirty-eight-year-old cotton broker named Alfred Brierley appeared to have gained 'the inside track' on Florence's affections.

On Thursday 21st March 1889, Florence arranged a liaison with Brierley at Flatman's Hotel, in London's West

End. Unfortunately, Brierley had the poor grace to inform her that he had love for another woman, which likely explains for their leaving the hotel abruptly the following morning. Whilst in the capital, Florence also sought the advice from a firm of London solicitors, hoping to arrange a divorce from her husband. She returned to Liverpool in time for the Grand National.

James Maybrick died on 11th May 1889. At the behest of his brother Michael, the corpse was subject to a port-mortem examination. By the time that the doctors where ready to lay down their instruments and remove their aprons, all three were agreed that the cause of death was administrant of an irritant poison. Battlecrease House, and James' offices at Tithebarn Street, were ransacked in search for any bottle, box, packet and stain suggestive of poison. On 19th May 1889, Florence was formally charged with the murder of her husband. The accusation had arisen principally from the suspicions of Michael Maybrick. Florence would never see her children again.

On 31st July 1889, the trial of Florence Elizabeth Maybrick opened in the court of St. George's Hall, Liverpool. The judge was Sir James Fitzjames Stephens. On 7th August, the jury returned after an absence of a mere thirty-five minutes. The verdict: guilty. Florence was sentenced to death.

After much public out-cry, the Home Secretary, Henry Matthews conceded that there remained reasonable doubt as to whether the arsenic found in James Maybrick's body was responsible for his death. Consequently, Florence's sentence was commuted to life imprisonment. She was thereafter transferred to Woking Convict Prison, serving fifteen years before finally achieving her release in 1904.

Returning to her homeland, Florence Maybrick ended her life as a recluse; living in a three-roomed cabin near South Kent, Connecticut. She died penniless and alone on 23rd October 1941 and was buried in the grounds of South Kent School.

Chapter 1

Michael Maybrick

Born:	31st January 1841, Liverpool
Parents:	William Maybrick, Susannah Wainwright
Spouse:	Laura Withers
Children:	None
Death:	26th August 1913, Buxton, Isle of Wight

Michael Maybrick was born in Liverpool to parents William & Susannah Maybrick, on 31st January 1841. At an early age he commenced a study of the piano forte, and when eight years old could play tolerably well on that instrument. He then began turning his attention to the organ, the 'king of instruments', and made such rapid progress that, at the age of fourteen he was appointed organist of St. Peter's, the parish church of Liverpool. It was eventually decided to give his musical abilities their full chance by sending him to Leipzig…and when he was twenty-two, he took his departure for the celebrated German Conservatoire. (Touchstone; Or the New Era, 14th September 1878).

Better known to the world by his nom de plume, Stephen Adams, Michael Maybrick became one of the most celebrated musicians of his day. By the late 1880's, Michael was at the zenith of his career, and at the high-end of London's elites. Forming a partnership with Bristol-born lawyer and lyricist Fred Weatherly, his most popular ballads included; 'The Warrior Bold', 'True Blue', 'True to Last', and most famously, 'Nancy Lee'. He also authored a lesser known, nautical ditty titled 'They All Love Jack'.

Like his elder brother James, who undoubtedly introduced him to the craft, Michael was an eminent Freemason. According to The Freemason, a periodical published by authority of the United Grand Lodge of England, Michael Maybrick was man in a powerful position; ascending to the very pinnacle of the fraternity's hierarchy. They wrote after his death in 1913;

A wide circle of Brethren will regret to learn of the death of Bro. Michael Maybrick…he was initiated in 1876, in the Athenaeum Lodge, No. 1491. In the following year he became a founder of the Orpheus Lodge, No. 1706, formed for members of the music profession. He was exalted in the Mount Sinai Royal Arch Chapter,

No. 19, in 1878...In the Ancient and Accepted Right he was perfected in the St. George Rose Croix Chapter, No. 42...In 1889 he was appointed Grand Organist of England, and also Grand Organist of Grand Chapter...In 1890, he was admitted a member of the thirtieth degree.

Known to his family as 'Blucher', fame and celebrity had so changed Michael that it was once said of him that; 'after he wrote 'The Holy City', he was floating on the celestial plains and did not belong to earth. He thought he should be classed with Shakespeare, Byron, Milton and Tennyson'. The family joke, from his younger brother Edwin, was that 'he had already engaged a tomb at Westminster Abbey.' It is recorded that, from the start, Florence found Michael to be uncomfortably cold and domineering, claiming that 'Michael had always had spite against her.'

In 2015, screenwriter Bruce Robinson released They All Love Jack, identifying Michael as the Whitechapel murderer. Based upon fifteen years of research, Robinson attributes a multitude of killings to Michael, including that of Johnny Gill in Bradford, and latterly his own brother, James.

Following his brother's death, Michael relocated to the Isle of Wight, where he served as mayor of Ryde for five consecutive terms. On the 9th March 1893, he married his forty-year-old housekeeper, Laura Withers. They were accompanied by his deceased brother's two children, James and Gladys Evelyn. Michael Maybrick died in his sleep of heart failure on 26th August 1913. Above his grave, on a large ornamental headstone is engraved the epitaph; 'There shall be no more death'.

CHAPTER 2

THE FLORENCE MAYBRICK TRIAL OF 1889 AND THE NEED FOR COURTS OF CRIMINAL APPEAL

BY KIERAN JAMES

Abstract: The criminal trial of Mrs. Florence Maybrick, held in Liverpool, England during the height of the British Empire 1889, is widely regarded as one of the greatest travesties of justice in British legal history where even the judge at the end of the trial remarked "well, they can't convict her on that evidence" and the chief prosecutor nodded his head in agreement. Mrs. Maybrick was tried for murdering her husband via arsenic poisoning. However, the trial became a morality trial when the learned judge, Mr. Justice James Fitzjames Stephen, linked Mrs. Maybrick's demonstrated adultery to her alleged desire to physically remove her husband by administering poison. The jury, which pronounced a guilty verdict, consisted of 12 untrained and unschooled men who were unable to grasp the technical evidence and were probably unduly influenced by the judge's summing-up and by the professional status of one of the medical witnesses for the prosecution. The case is a timely reminder today for an international audience of the fallibility and inherent weaknesses of the legal system and the desperate need to retain Courts of Criminal Appeal within the courts system.

1: Introduction

The criminal trial of Mrs. Florence Maybrick, held in Liverpool, England during the height of the British Empire 1889, is widely regarded as one of the greatest travesties of justice in British legal history where even the judge at the end of the trial remarked *"well, they can't convict her on that evidence"* and the chief prosecutor nodded his head in agreement [as witnessed by a newspaper reporter and cited in Christie, (19680, p.141)]. Mrs. Maybrick was tried for murdering her husband via arsenic poisoning. However, the trial became a morality trial when the learned judge, Mr. Justice James Fitzjames Stephen, linked Mrs. Maybrick's demonstrated adultery to her alleged desire to physically remove her husband by administering poison. Mr. Justice Stephen was wrong to attempt to, in the words of his brother Sir Leslie, turn his own criminal court into a 'school of morality' [cited in Christie, (1968), p.134]. The jury, which pronounced a guilty verdict, consisted of twelve untrained and unschooled men who were unable to grasp the technical evidence and were probably unduly influenced by the judge's summing-up and by the professional status of one of the medical witnesses for the prosecution.

Szijártó (2002, p.212) writes that the advantages of microhistory such as the present paper are as follows: *"...it can appeal to its readers by being interesting, it transmits lived experience, it stands on both feet on the ground of reality, and with all the lines branching out from the event, person or community in focus, it points towards the general".* The case presented here is a timely reminder today for an international audience of the fallibility and inherent weaknesses of the legal system and the desperate need to retain Courts of Criminal Appeal within the courts system. It also suggests that senior judges aged over 55 years, and especially those who have suffered strokes or head injuries, need to be regularly evaluated by their peers or by other qualified persons. Mental decline can occur earlier than expected and can have disastrous consequences.

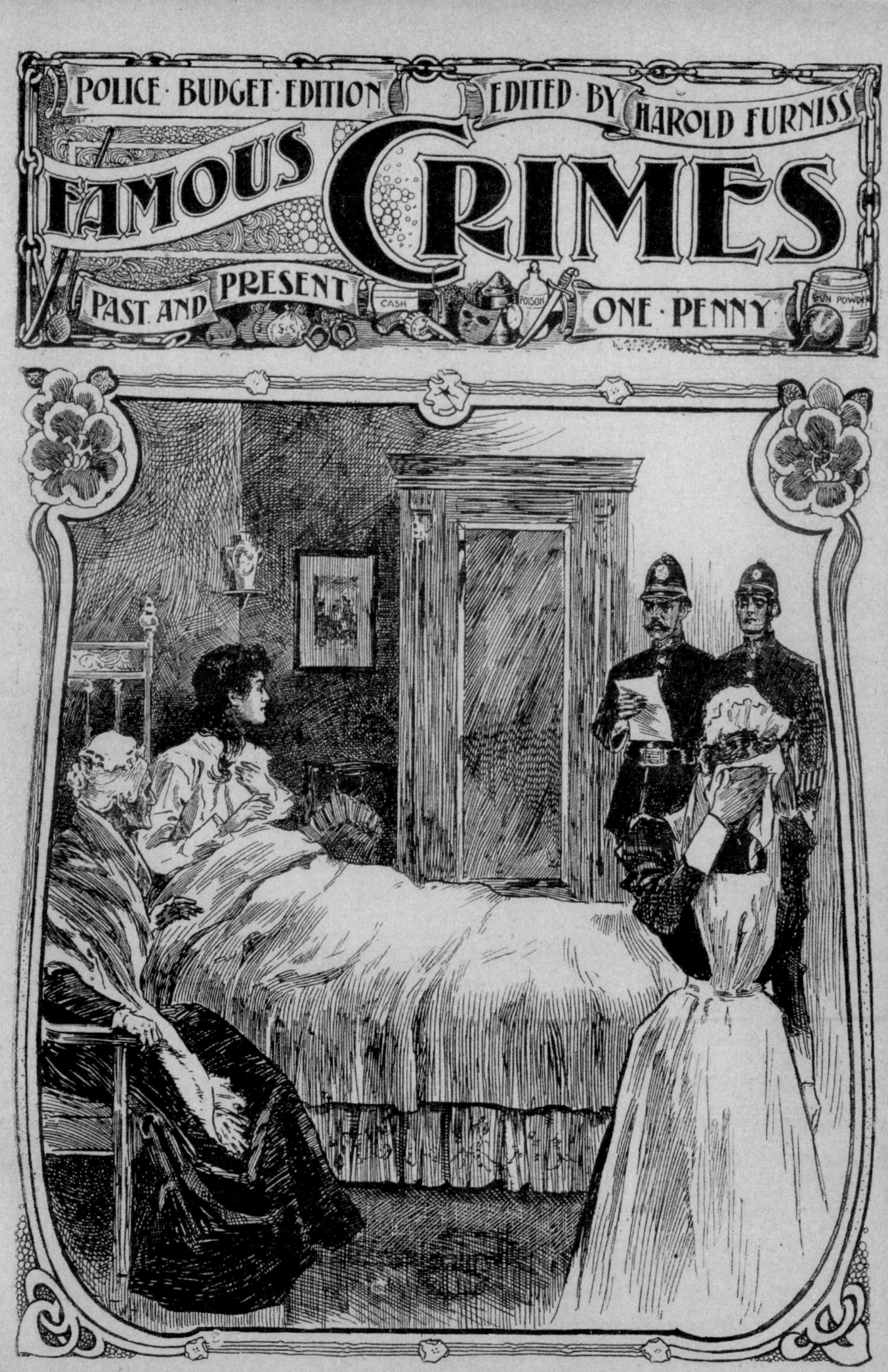

MRS. MAYBRICK ARRESTED BY SUPERINTENDENT BRYNING.

Chapter 2

2: James and Florence Maybrick – the initial meeting and early married life

1881. Marriage solemnized at the Church in the Parish of St. James's, Westminster, in the County of ~~London~~ Middlesex

No.	When Married.	Name and Surname.	Age.	Condition.	Rank or Profession.	Residence at time of Marriage.	Father's Name and Surname.	Rank or Profession of Father.
32	July 27 1881	James Maybrick	full	Bachelor	Esquire	S. James's	William Maybrick	Gentleman (dec)
		Florence Elizabeth Chandler	a minor	Spinster		Paris	William George Chandler	Banker (dec)

Married in the Church, according to the Rites and Ceremonies of the Established Church, by Licence or after —— by me J. Dyer Tovey Preacher & Assistant

This Marriage was solemnized between us, James Maybrick, Florence Elizabeth Chandler; in the Presence of us, Michael Maybrick, Baroness Caroline E von Roques

I hereby certify that the above is a true Extract from the Register Book of Marriages belonging to the Parish of St. James's, Westminster.

Witness my Hand this 28th Day of April 1902. T. Eaton Cornick. Curate

MRS MAYBRICK'S MARRIAGE CERTIFICATE.

James and Florence's Marriage Certificate - Image courtesy of Rob Clack

Mr. James Maybrick, cotton merchant of Liverpool, was an eligible bachelor in his early-40s when he met the 17-year-old American Miss Florence 'Florie' Elizabeth Chandler on board the steamer SS Baltic heading back from the USA to England which had departed from New York City on 11 March 1880 [Christie, (1968), p.36; Feldman, (2007), pp.75–76; Graham and Emmas, (1999), p.28; Harrison, (2008), p.219]. Whilst gathered around the bar on the first evening offshore, Mr. Maybrick was introduced by General J.G. Hazard of New Orleans to the Baroness von Roques and her daughter Florence [Christie, (1968), p.37; Graham and Emmas, (1999), p.28][1]. Mr. Maybrick had been in the New World to attend to his cotton interests. Maybrick & Co. had opened an American office in the cotton-exporting port-city of Norfolk, Virginia in the late-1870s [Graham and Emmas, (1999), p.31]. Christie (1968, p.37) was not over-exaggerating his point when he wrote that the introduction of James to Florence by General Hazard "set in motion a portentous train of events". To the surprise of many observers, James and Florence began a romance which had crystallised into a committed relationship by the time the ship arrived in Liverpool six days after its departure. When they left the ship it was decided that if they still felt the same way about each other in a year's time they would marry [Graham and Emmas, (1999), p.32][2]. This criteria must have been fulfilled because the couple duly wed in St. James's Church (which still stands today) in London's Piccadilly on 27 July 1881 when Florence was only 18-years-old [Christie, (1968), p.38; Feldman, (2007), p.76; Graham and Emmas, (1999), p.34; Maybrick, (2012), p.21]. Christie (1968, p.39) offers the following observations about the marriage which seemed to begin favourably but soon deteriorated amidst adultery and arsenic addiction:

"As events unfolded it is now clear that the marriage was founded in part on avarice and deception. While unquestionably sincere in his affections [how can Christie, from the vantage point of 1968, be so sure about this point?], James was intrigued by the Baroness's glib tales of a vast tract of Southern lands that would some day be inherited by her daughter. The mother, for her part, was nearing the end of her financial rope and envisioned a life of ease in her twilight years with the aid of a seemingly rich son-in-law. Genuinely in love for the first time [how can Christie, from the vantage point of 1968, be so sure about this point also?], Florie was an innocent pawn in the game – dominated by her mother, bedazzled by her bridegroom."

After briefly honeymooning in Bournemouth they lived in Norfolk for the next three years, spending about half their time in USA and the other half in Liverpool [Christie, (1968), p.40]. In 1884, James Maybrick was replaced by his brother Edwin as the buying agent for Maybrick & Co. in Norfolk, and James Maybrick's family returned to Liverpool [Christie, (1968), p.40; Graham and Emmas, (1999), pp.38–39]. They first rented a house known as Beechville in the suburb of Grassendale Park North [Christie, 1968), p.40; Graham and Emmas, (1999), p.39]. The family later took out a five-year lease on Battlecrease House in Aigburth, near the Mersey

River, Liverpool, in February1888 [Graham and Emmas, (1999), pp.43–44]. According to Christie (1968, p.41), and there can be no dissenting opinions here, "it was [at Battlecrease House] that fate would strike". The couple brought with them to the ill-fated Battlecrease House (which still stands today on Riversdale Road) their two children the elder Master James Chandler Maybrick ('Bobo') (born 24 March 1882) [Christie, (1968), p.41; Graham and Emmas, (1999), p.39, note; Maybrick, (2012), p.21] and the younger Miss Gladys Evelyn Maybrick [born 20 June 1886, according to Maybrick, (2012), p.21; and 21 June 1886, according to Graham and Emmas, (1999), p.39].

Christie (1968, p.42) comments that "[i]n an age dedicated to the worship of property and material things it is significant that Maybrick, despite his high position in the world of trade, never owned a home throughout his married life". The Maybricks were much like the 'new money' Forsytes (although the Forsytes were richer than the Maybricks) in the novel *The Forsyte Saga,* always being concerned with the maintenance of the appearances befitting a family of high social standing. As Christie (1968, p.42) commented: "from all appearances in the first years of their marriage the Maybricks were safely embarked on the conventional social life of Victorian England". An important reason for the Maybricks' endless whirl of dinner-parties was no doubt to impress their business and social acquaintances. Mr. Maybrick's attitude towards his arsenic eating reflected the hypocrisies of the times, with him swinging from boasting about it to angrily denying it depending on the person he was talking to and the immediate context. For example, when Florie wrote to James' younger brother Michael in March 1889 to advise him that James was taking a 'white powder' which might explain the pains in his head, James angrily responded to Michael's questioning about the powder with: "Whoever told you that? It is a damned lie" [cited in Christie, (1968), pp.48–49].

Mr. and Mrs. Maybrick's marital relationship worsened during their time at Battlecrease House when it was put under considerable strain by Mr. Maybrick's financial problems, his arsenic habits, his infidelity [Edwards, (2007), p.54], his aloofness, the couple's spending habits, and Mrs. Maybrick's personal debts. Sometime during 1887 Florie discovered that James was regularly seeing and maintaining a mistress and it was from this point onwards that the Maybricks slept in separate beds [Christie, (1968), p.45].

Mr. Maybrick almost certainly had an arsenic addiction; the eating of arsenic by middle-class men as a medicinal or sexual tonic seems to have been a 19th century phenomenon. A brief, signed by Charles Russell QC, I. Fletcher Moulton QC, Harry Bookin Poland QC, and Reginald Smith QC, at Lincoln's Inn on 12 April 1892, and prepared by Messrs. Lumley and Lumley presents evidence that a Mr. Valentine Charles Blake signed a statutory declaration to the effect that he had procured for Mr. Maybrick 150 grains of arsenic around two months before his (Maybrick's) death [cited in Maybrick, (2012), pp.278, footnote, pp.312–313]. Mary Howard of Norfolk, Virginia, the madam of a brothel Mr. Maybrick patronised at least three times a week for several years prior to his marriage, spoke as follows about Mr. Maybrick's arsenic eating: "I saw him frequently in his different moods and fancies". He took arsenic two or three times each evening, she swore, and she was afraid that he would die on the premises and "some of us [the house girls] would be suspected of his murder" [cited in Christie, (1968), p.36]. Thomas Stansell, a black servant of Maybrick's from his bachelor days in Norfolk (1878–1880), also testified to Maybrick's arsenic habit but it seems that this witness failed to receive the respect he deserved in court perhaps for race-related reasons. Stansell testified that, in his first year of service, he was asked three or four times to go the drug-store and buy arsenic for Maybrick without a prescription [Christie, (1968), p.119].

Mr. Maybrick's health progressively deteriorated in late April 1889 and his death on 11 May 1889 of exhaustion caused by gastro-enteritis [Graham and Emmas, (1999), p.173; Lumley and Lumley-prepared brief cited in Maybrick, (2012), p.268, p.309, p.335) could have been influenced by the effects of arsenic withdrawal. The quantity of arsenic found in his body post-mortem, one-tenth of a grain total in the liver, kidney, and intestines, was consistent with an arsenic eater who had left off the habit for some time perhap's even for a couple of months [Christie, (1968), p.70; Feldman, 2007; Lumley and Lumley-prepared brief cited in Maybrick, (2012), p.336]. The gastro-enteritis which killed Mr. Maybrick was probably caused by bad food or drink or by excessive consumption of the same or by Mr. Maybrick's distressing experience of being soaked wet on the day of the Wirral Races, 27 April 1889 [Graham and Emmas, (1999), p.173; Lumley and Lumley-prepared brief cited in Maybrick, (2012), p.266, p.268, p.309]. The effects of arsenic withdrawal may well have been a factor in his death [Christie, (1968), p.167]. In fact, Christie (1968, p.167) calls this the 'most sensible theory' yet advanced about the cause of death.

3: Key participants at the Florence Maybrick trial

For the first nine decades of the 20th century James and Florence Maybrick were remembered because of the notorious 1889 criminal trial of the American Florence when she was convicted of murdering her older English husband James by arsenic poisoning (Schoettler, 1993). During the trial, the jury and court reflected on the salacious details of her affair with Alfred Brierley and the trial was widely regarded as a trial of Mrs. Maybrick's morality. Consistent with the ethos of Victorian times Mr. Maybrick's extra-marital relationships [Edwards, (2007), p.54] were glossed over while those of his wives were viewed as unforgivable [Christie, (1968), pp.126–127; Graham and Emmas, (1999), p.7]. It was easy for many people of the era to believe that a woman capable of committing adultery was easily capable of committing murder as well. In fact, the aging Mr. Justice James Fitzjames Stephen (born 3 March 1829–died 11 March 1894) (father of 'Jack-the-Ripper' serial-murder suspect James Kenneth Stephen, 25 February 1859–3 February 1892) presented the case to the jury specifically as a *morality trial* (as we shall see). Generally, it is perceived that the defence erred in not asking for the trial to be moved away from Liverpool [Graham and Emmas, (1999), p.156], as Mrs. Maybrick had requested in a letter to her mother from Walton Jail (dated 28 June 1889) [Maybrick, (2012), p.51]. However, Mrs. Maybrick herself suggested in her 1904 book *My Fifteen Lost Years* that the reason had been a funding shortfall [Graham and Emmas, (1999), pp.157–158; Maybrick, (2012), p.51].

Charles Russell (Barrister for the defense) & Sir James Steven (Judge)

Charles Russell (10 November 1832–10 August 1900) (later Baron Russell of Killowen and Lord Chief Justice of England) was Mrs. Maybrick's famed defence lawyer and a strong supporter of her innocence {although at the time this was denied by certain commentators belonging to the anti-Florence Maybrick camp including Lord Hugh Cecil [Maybrick, (2012), p.144, p.255]}. Christie (1968, p.72) remarks that Sir Charles: "was regarded by most authorities as the most brilliant advocate of his day". Confirming this assertion, he rose to the pinnacle of the English legal system, the Lord Chief Justice of England. However, Sir Charles performed only moderately well in defence of Mrs. Maybrick. The reason for this was that he was mentally exhausted following his important role in the earlier Parnell Commission hearings which had included his finest hour, a six day defence speech [Christie, (1968), p.111; Graham and Emmas, (1999), p.161]. His biographer O'Brien (1901, p.259) wrote that: "to dwell on any of Russell's cases after the Parnell Commission would be an anti-climax" but he does spend five pages at this juncture on the Maybrick trial. Mrs. Maybrick was later to call Sir Charles, who visited her in Aylesbury Prison, "the noblest, truest friend that woman ever had"; "the champion of the weak and the oppressed"; and "the brave upholder of justice and law in the face of prejudice and public hostility" [Maybrick, (2012), pp.143–144]. Sir Charles' direct opponent at the Florence Maybrick trial was Mr. John Edmund Wentworth Addison QC MP (5 November 1838–22 April 1907).

Mr. Justice Stephen exhibited signs of approaching insanity during the trial and he was widely regarded as being only a shadow of his former self [Graham and Emmas, (1999), p.193; Maybrick, (2012), p.237, p.393]. He was forced to resign in April 1891 [Christie, (1968), p.145; Graham and Emmas, (1999), p.193; Maybrick, (2012), p.393] and he died on 11 March 1894 in a private lunatic asylum in Ipswich (so clearly Mrs. Maybrick (2012, p.237) was wrong when she wrote in 1904 that he died 'a year' after her trial) [Christie, (1968), p.145; Graham and Emmas, (1999), p.193]. He was called 'the great mad judge' in the Liverpool Daily Post of 13 August 1900 [cited in Maybrick, (2012), p.238]. This Daily Post article concluded that "[i]t was shocking to think that a human life depended upon the direction of this wreck of what was once a great judge" [cited in Maybrick, (2012), p.239]. In the 1890 second edition of his book A General View of the Criminal Law of England Mr. Justice Stephen was to write that the Florence Maybrick case was the only case out of the 979 he had tried between January 1885 and September 1889 where "there could be any doubt about the facts" [Stephen, (1890), p.174, Christie, (1968), p.145; Maybrick, (2012), p.394].

Mr. Justice Stephen's closing address in the Florence Maybrick trial was an oddity in that he was favourable to Mrs. Maybrick on the first afternoon but inexplicably changed his tone when he began again the next morning [Christie, (1968), p.19, p.137; Graham and Emmas, (1999), p.5; Lumley and Lumley-prepared brief cited in Maybrick, (2012), p.364; Maybrick, (2012), p.393]. It was the closing day section of Mr. Justice Stephen's address which was ultimately the one factor which was crucial in the failure of Sir Charles to secure his client's acquittal [Edwards, (2007), p.54]. Ultimately Mrs. Maybrick was found guilty based on nothing more than "the mere gossip of servants" [Maybrick, (2012), p.41]. Christie (1968, p.56, p.57) concludes as follows about the shadowy coalition below-stairs who were waiting for Mrs. Maybrick to trip up so that they might conspire to do her harm:

"It is undoubtedly true, however, that an amorphous, loosely organized cabal was operating at Battlecrease House to snare Florie in some misdeed that would break up her marriage and deprive her of her children; but, whatever its objective, it was certainly not to hound her to the gallows...Over the span of fifteen days from Saturday, April 27th [1889] to Saturday May 11th, this deadly cabal did its work at Battlecrease House."

Christie (1968, p.56) lists Mrs. Briggs, "abetted by her married and unmarried sisters", a group of women who had earlier held romantic aspirations in relation to both James and Alfred Brierley but who had remained friends of the family and were frequent visitors to Battlecrease. The aptly-named Miss Alice Yapp was also named by Christie, a nosy domestic-servant who opened a letter of Mrs. Maybrick's she had been given for the purpose of posting it to Brierley on the pretext that three-year-old Gladys had dropped it in the mud. Alice Yapp was arguably bitter after suffering a recent relationship breakup of her own. Miss Yap brought the letter to Edwin Maybrick who telegraphed his brother Michael with instructions to come to the house straight away from London [Christie (1968), p.61]. Miss Yapp was also the one who reported to Mrs. Briggs seeing flypapers in the bathroom and these were later tested for arsenic. In a recent murder trial in Liverpool two working-class women had been convicted for murder by obtaining arsenic from flypaper. On the same day as the two previously mentioned events, Miss Yap telegraphed Michael Maybrick with the message: "come at once strange things going on here" [Christie, (1968), p.61].

Drs. Carter and Humphreys were ready and willing to write out 'acute inflammation of the stomach' on the death certificate but only decided not to do so after a discussion with Michael where Mrs. Maybrick was implicated [Christie, (1968), p.70, pp.99–101]. We then had the strange situation of a musical composer advising two medical practitioners as to the cause of death [letter from family friend Charles Ratcliff to John Aunspaugh, May/June 1889, cited in Christie, (1968), pp.63–64]. After the cross-examination of Dr. Humphreys at the trial, Christie (1968, p.100) remarks that "[t]here were strong doubts [among those assembled in the courtroom] as to how far Michael Maybrick and his suspicions had swayed the doctor in withholding a certificate of death". At Michael's insistence, James' body was exhumed two weeks after its burial but, as mentioned earlier, only one-tenth of a grain was found in the kidney, liver, and intestines and none in the rest of the body [Christie, (1968), p.70].

4: My analysis of the Florence Maybrick trial

Mrs. Maybrick was found guilty largely based on the flypaper containing arsenic [Edwards, (2007), p.54]. She claimed that she was using this recipe as a facial treatment (Schoettler, 1993). Lumley and Lumley noted that: "[t]he purchase and soaking of fly-papers is the only direct evidence of the possession of arsenic in any form by Mrs. Maybrick" [Maybrick, (2012), p.269]. After she was imprisoned her mother found such a fly-paper recipe dated 1878 inside Mrs. Maybrick's family Bible, which was cited by the Lumley and Lumley-prepared brief [cited in Maybrick, (2012), pp.347–348) as additional evidence in favour of her innocence. This prescription for face-wash containing arsenic was signed by a Dr. Bay of New York City [Christie, (1968), pp.216–217; Maybrick, (2012), p.348]. It was duly made up by a French chemist in Paris on 17 July 1878 [Christie, (1968), pp.216–217; Maybrick, (2012), p.348]. Unfortunately, this information was received far too late for the original trial and the authorities consistently rejected appeals for a new trial. Other evidence unfavourable to Florence included: the finding of arsenic in meat juice (half a grain); on a handkerchief; on a dressing-gown; in a bottle; and in a package labelled 'arsenic: poison for cats' [Christie, (1968), p.102]. The handkerchief; dressing-gown; bottle; and package were all found in the defendant's bedroom [Christie, (1968), p.102]. The amounts ranged from a fraction of a grain to 65 grains [Christie, (1968), p.102], but are also consistent with self-medication of arsenic by James. The ridiculous inscription on the package 'arsenic: poison for cats' strongly suggests a sick joke and possible malicious intent on the part of the domestic servants.

The following somewhat strange statement by the Home Secretary, Mr. Henry Matthews (13 January 1826–3 April 1913), was the ground for the 1889 decision to spare Mrs. Maybrick the death penalty and reduce her sentence to life imprisonment:

"After the fullest consideration, and after taking the best medical and legal advice that could be obtained, the Home Secretary [H.M.] advised her majesty [Queen Victoria] to respite the capital punishment of Florence Elizabeth Maybrick and to commute the punishment to penal servitude for life; inasmuch as, although the evidence leads to the conclusion that the prisoner administered and attempted to administer arsenic to her husband with intent to murder him, yet it does not wholly exclude a reasonable doubt whether his death was in fact caused by the administration of arsenic."

[cited in Maybrick, (2012), pp.226–227, emphasis original].

As Maybrick (2012) explains, there are a number of major problems raised by this statement. Firstly, if there was indeed 'reasonable doubt' (a legal term) whether James Maybrick's death *was in fact caused by the administration of arsenic* then the prisoner Mrs. Maybrick should have been found 'not guilty' by the jury and should have been immediately set free rather than simply have had her sentence reduced to life imprisonment [Henry W. Lucy, *The Strand Magazine,* London, November 1900, cited in Maybrick, (2012), p.253]. Henry Matthews was indeed trying to claim some totally untenable middle ground. For the jury to have found Mrs. Maybrick guilty, all of the following pre-conditions should have been satisfied:

a) that Mr. Maybrick's death was caused by arsenic poisoning
b) that Mrs. Maybrick administered the fatal dose of arsenic
c) that the arsenic was administered by Mrs. Maybrick with the intent to kill [Christie, (1968), p.113].

If only pre-conditions (a) and (b) were present then Mrs. Maybrick could have been convicted on a lesser charge but not on the charge of murder. In fact, there were serious doubts associated with each of the three necessary pre-conditions and it can well be argued that none of the three pre-conditions, even taken as individual propositions, were ever proved beyond reasonable doubt. In regards pre-condition (a), taken by itself, if over 65 grains of arsenic were found in the house how can we explain why such a tiny quantity of arsenic was found in the body of the deceased? Even if the Home Office's statement that "although the evidence leads to the conclusion that the prisoner administered and attempted to administer arsenic to her husband with intent to murder him" was valid [which it was not (Lumley and Lumley-prepared brief cited in Maybrick, (2012), p.296)] this should not have been enough to have sustained a murder charge because the death had not been proven beyond reasonable doubt to have been caused by arsenic poisoning [Maybrick, (2012), p.244]. Even Mr. Justice Stephen, although on the whole a poor performer at the trial, had told the members of the jury that *"[i]t is essential to this charge that the man died of arsenic"* [cited in Maybrick, (2012), p.227, emphasis original].

Secondly, Mrs. Maybrick was never tried at court for "administering and attempting to administer arsenic... with intent to murder" her husband (Lumley and Lumley prepared brief cited in Maybrick, (2012), p.365] so she could not and should not have been found guilty of such a charge [Christie, (1968), p.170; Maybrick, (2012), p.228]. This was the charge which the Home Office perhaps wished or imagined that Mrs. Maybrick had been charged with.

The medical evidence made it clear that the quantity of arsenic contained in Mr. Maybrick's body – one-tenth of a grain – was insufficient to have caused death [Maybrick, (2012), p.235; Lumley and Lumley-prepared brief cited in Maybrick, (2012), pp.313–314]. Mr. Davies found 0.02 of a grain in the liver and Dr. Stevenson found 0.076 of a grain in the liver and 0.015 in the intestines making the total amount found by both doctors combined around one-tenth of a grain [Graham and Emmas, (1999), p.173; Lumley and Lumley-prepared brief cited in Maybrick, (2012), p.311]. The smallest quantity of arsenic previously found to have caused a victim's death had been two grains and this was with respect to a woman who had not been an arsenic eater during life [Lumley and Lumley-prepared brief cited in Maybrick, (2012), p.311]. The experienced doctors for the defence (Dr. Stevenson excepted) were of the opinion that the low quantity of arsenic found in Mr. Maybrick's body was consistent with 'administration in medicinal doses, and [the arsenic] might have been introduced a considerable time before [death]' [Maybrick, (2012), p.235 and see also Lumley and Lumley-prepared brief cited in Maybrick, (2012), p.313]. In other words, the evidence merely showed that Mr. Maybrick had been self-administering arsenic and that he may have stopped doing so (with disastrous consequences) some time prior to his eventual demise.

We should now briefly refer to the sub-standard responses from the star expert witness for the prosecution, Dr. Thomas Stevenson {a lecturer on forensic medicine and chemistry at Guy's Hospital [Christie, (1968), p.107]}, under cross-examination in the courtroom. The evidence also shows how deeply divided the doctors in this case were. In response to a question from QC Addison for the prosecution, the witness answered as follows: "I have no doubts that this man died from the effects of arsenic" [cited in Christie, (1968), p.108]. It is worth following the cross-examination responses closely. When he was then asked about the fatal dose of arsenic needed to kill an adult he responded: "two grains or thereabouts" [cited in Christie, (1968), p.108]. Then it was Sir Charles' turn to cross-examine. Christie (1986, p.109) remarks that: "Sir Charles realised he had a formidable witness on his hands", but the reference to 'formidable' should be held to refer to his overall self-confident presence rather than to the quality of his answers. Sir Charles asked whether there is any 'distinct symptom' of arsenic poisoning which distinguishes it from gastroenteritis caused by other factors. Dr. Stevenson was snide and over-confident when he replied: "there is no distinctive diagnostic symptom of arsenical poisoning: *the diagnostic thing is finding the arsenic*". We see here the doctor falling into the careful trap laid by the expert defence counsel. Sir Charles let his case rest when he then got Dr. Stevenson to confess that 0.076 of a grain of arsenic was found in the liver and 0.015 of a grain in the intestines, totaling 0.091 of a grain. Clearly then, given that the diagnostic thing is finding the arsenic, there was no evidence at all that Mr. Maybrick died from arsenic poisoning. As Christie (1968, p.110) concludes: "if two grains of the poison is a fatal dose on the average, as the witness had testified, it is not surprising that many in the court felt that such minute traces of arsenic represented rather feeble evidence on which to base the doctor's opinion as to the cause of death". Sir Charles could be forgiven if he believed that this time he had landed the case's decisive blow. In contrast to the testimony of Dr. Stevenson, Dr. Charles Tidy of the London Hospital {who held a position comparable to Dr. Stevenson's at Guy's [Christie, (1968), p.115]} and Dr. Frank T. Paul, medical authority at University College, Liverpool and Victoria University, Manchester, both argued that it was *not* a case of arsenic poisoning; Dr. Tidy said the case "absolutely points away from arsenic as the cause of death" while Dr. Paul testified that "[t]he post-mortem appearances do not show that it was set up by arsenic" [cited in Christie,(1968), p.117].

On the second and concluding day of his summing-up, Mr. Justice Stephen told the jury as follows:

"You must consider the case as a mere medical case, in which you are to decide whether the man did or did not die of arsenic according to the medical evidence. You must not consider it as a mere chemical case, in which you decide whether the man died from arsenic which was discovered as the result of a chemical analysis. You must decide it as a great, high, and important case, involving in itself not only medical and chemical questions, but embodying in itself a most highly important moral question – and by that term, moral question, I do not mean a question of what is right and wrong in a moral point of view, but questions in which human nature enters and in which you must rely on your knowledge of human nature in determining the resolution you arrive at."

"I could say a good many other things about the awful nature of the charge, but I do not think it will be necessary to do any one thing. Your own hearts must tell you what it is for a person to go on administering poison to a helpless, sick man, upon whom she has already inflicted a dreadful injury – an injury fatal to married life; the person who could do such a thing as that must be destitute of the least trace of human feeling... We have to consider this not in an unfeeling spirit – far from it – but in the spirit of people resolved to solve by intellectual means an intellectual problem of great difficulty"

[cited in Maybrick, (2012), pp.319–321, emphasis original].

This extraordinarily incoherent, muddled, and problematic set of statements, which was very influential in determining Mrs. Maybrick's eventual fate, deserves careful study. In the first sentence the statement appears to begin well but it immediately deteriorates in quality from that point onwards, and doubles back to contradict itself. Instead of the above incoherent statements, the judge instead should have asked the jurors to reflect upon three straight-forward questions and three straight-forward questions only [Lumley and Lumley-prepared brief cited in Maybrick, (2012), p.321]:

a) Did Mr. Maybrick die of arsenic poisoning?
b) Did Mrs. Maybrick administer arsenic to Mr. Maybrick?
c) Did she do so with the intent to kill?

Mr. Justice Stephen's last-quoted statement that the members of the jury must *solve* by *intellectual means an intellectual problem of great difficulty* (emphasis original) seems faintly ridiculous given that the medical evidence clearly indicated that Mr. Maybrick's body contained around one-tenth of a grain of arsenic and the smallest quantity ever known to have killed someone was two grains (or 20 times as much). It hardly seems an intellectual feat of staggering proportions for someone to conclude that there was reasonable doubt that Mr. Maybrick did not die of arsenic poisoning.

What is especially interesting in Mr. Justice Stephen's statements is that he directly informed the uneducated laymen of the jury to disregard the expert medical testimony of the experienced doctors for the defence including Dr. Tidy and Dr. Paul. This is the interpretation which I give to the following sentence: "you must not consider it as a *mere chemical case*, in which you decide whether the man died from arsenic which was discovered as the result of a chemical analysis" (emphasis original). When this sentence is taken out of the convoluted paragraph in which it first appears its inappropriateness is even starker. Instead of giving due weight to the medical evidence, Mr. Justice Stephen instead referred the members of the jury to a *most highly important moral question (emphasis original) where they must rely on your [their] knowledge of human nature. In other words, Mr. Justice Stephen set this case up as a trial of the morality of Mrs. Maybrick.* He then stated that "she has already inflicted a dreadful injury – an injury fatal to married life" upon Mr. Maybrick. He was thus explicitly encouraging the jurors to regard Mrs. Maybrick's adultery and her husband's strange death while she was nursing him as connected sordid pieces of the same morality play. The adultery was specifically portrayed as relevant. By encouraging the jurors to *rely on your [their] knowledge of human nature* (emphasis original)

Mr. Justice Stephen appeared to be implying that the 'human nature' of someone who had inflicted the injury of adultery upon her husband would incline that same person to want to remove her husband's presence physically so as to begin a new life with her lover. However, Mr. Justice Stephen ignored the facts that the Brierley affair had long since ended and that Mrs. Maybrick could simply have divorced her husband and in fact had already taken some steps in that direction [Maybrick, (2012), p.365]. QC Addison, on behalf of the prosecution, had earlier set the deadly wheels in motion when he had (reprehensibly) claimed that Mrs. Maybrick "had so interwoven her adultery with her conduct that it was impossible to treat it as an ordinary case of adultery and not treat it as having any actual connection with the alleged crime" [cited in Christie, (1968), p.131].

Mr. Justice Stephen was clearly on a dangerous course when he instructed the jurors to listen to "[y]our [their] own hearts [which] must tell you [them] what it is for a person to go on *administering poison* to a helpless, sick man, upon whom she has already inflicted a dreadful injury" (emphasis original). Given that it was an all-male jury (Graham and Emmas, 1999) (women jurors were first used in England in 1920) the appeal for them to effectively listen to their emotions was clearly inflammatory and most prejudicial to Mrs. Maybrick's cause. Mr. Justice Stephen was effectively asking the jurors to put themselves in Mr. Maybrick's shoes, imagine that it was their wives who had betrayed them personally, and then to feel the full gamut of emotions which such circumstances would engender. Clearly, in such a context, a man's own adultery would not be relevant and Mr. Justice Stephen in the above quoted statements did not refer to it. Mrs. Maybrick (2012, p.236) wrote that "[t] he jury belonged to a class of men who were not competent to weigh technical evidence", and so direct pleas by Mr. Justice Stephen to the emotions of the jurors would most likely have been powerfully effective 3. Despite the case producing nearly 800,000 words of testimony it took the jurors only 38 minutes to reach their guilty verdict [Christie, (1968), p.20]. Another basic factual error made by Mr. Justice Stephen was to say "you have been convicted by a jury of this city" [cited in Christie, (1968), p.20]. The jury members were from Lancashire County but not from the city of Liverpool. One of the judge's more serious factual errors, which even the crown counsel was forced to correct him on, was to state that the reconciliation between husband and wife had taken place before (rather than after) Florence's overnight tryst with Brierley at Flatman's Hotel in London [Christie, (1968), p.139].

Lastly, there was no evidence presented at the trial which conclusively proved that Mrs. Maybrick had administered arsenic or any other poison to her late husband, and Mr. Justice Stephen clearly erred by suggesting that such evidence had been presented. The statement "the person who could do such a thing as that must be destitute of the least trace of human feeling" clearly suggests a morality trial where the judge had already found the prisoner guilty before the jurors had even left the courtroom to begin their deliberations. It seems that Mrs. Maybrick was found guilty by the judge of harbouring a certain state of alleged inner wickedness rather than because of actual proven actions or actual physical evidence. There is also an obvious ambiguity in that the judge's statement that "the person who could do such a thing as that" could reasonably be held to be referring back to *either* the adultery of Mrs. Maybrick or to her alleged administration of poison to her late husband. The ambiguity suggests that both the adultery and the alleged administration of poison were both seen by the judge as consistent with and indicative of the certain state of alleged wickedness which I claim the judge was imputing to Mrs. Maybrick. Mr. Justice Stephen's brother Sir Leslie, in his biography of his brother, remarked that James (Stephen) was a 'moralist in the old-fashioned sense' and that "he took advantage of his strength to carry out his own ideals of a criminal court as a school of morality" [cited in Christie, (1968), p.134].

Mr. Justice Stephen also mentioned a dog that had apparently died of arsenic poisoning, although there was no trace of arsenic in its body post-mortem, either not realising or not caring that arsenic would work its way through a dog's system much quicker than it would a man's [Lumley and Lumley-prepared brief cited in Maybrick, (2012), p.323]. The judge turned himself into an impromptu witness for the prosecution during his closing address; his ill-advised statements were of such a nature that any defence lawyer would have torn them to shreds. However, Sir Charles was not given this opportunity. The judge at the end of the trial remarked: "well, they can't convict her on that evidence" and the chief prosecutor, QC Addison, nodded his head to agree [as allegedly witnessed by a newspaper reporter and cited in Christie, (1968), p.141]. At the end of the trial Sir Charles was overheard saying to his fellow barristers in the corridors of St. George's Hall: "mark what I say, it is the most dangerous verdict that has ever been recorded in my experience" [cited in Graham and Emmas,

(1999), p.9]. Within half an hour of the trial ending, a petition against the verdict was signed by every junior barrister and by every Queen's Counsel present at the Assize Courts that day [Graham and Emmas, (1999), p.9].

Although many informed commentators at the time, including Sir Charles, and afterwards suggested that Mrs. Maybrick had been wrongly convicted [Beadle, 2005a; Maybrick, (2012), p.225] there was no Court of Criminal Appeal at that time. Mrs. Maybrick (2012, p.89) wrote in 1904 that "[t]he supineness of Parliament in not establishing a court of criminal appeal fastens a dark blot upon the judicature of England, and is inconsistent with the innate love of justice and fair play of its people". Other notable advocates for a Court of Criminal Appeal were Lord Esher in *The Times* of 17 August 1889 and *The Times* newspaper itself of the same date [Maybrick, (2012), p.260]. A Court of Criminal Appeal was eventually established by the Criminal Appeal Act 1907 [Christie, (1968), p.266]. The Florence Maybrick case is a timely reminder today for an international audience of the fallibility and inherent weaknesses of the legal system and the desperate need to retain Courts of Criminal Appeal within the courts system.

AFTER TWENTY-THREE YEARS—
MRS. MAYBRICK LANDING IN NEW YORK

5: Later life of Mrs. Maybrick

As mentioned, Mrs. Maybrick's death sentence was nearly immediately reduced to life imprisonment on the directions of the Home Office [Adamson, (1993), p.6; Edwards, (2007), p.54; Maybrick, (2012), p.60; O'Brien, (1901), p.259]. Sir Charles continued to lobby the Home Office for Florence's release up until his death in 1900. As O'Brien (1901, p.263) wrote: "and so, to the end, the fate of this unhappy woman occupied his thoughts, and he never ceased, either in private or officially, to say that there had been a grave miscarriage of justice in the case, and that Florence Maybrick 'ought to be allowed to go free'". Mrs. Maybrick was transferred from Woking Prison to Aylesbury Prison on 4 November 1896 [Christie, (1968), p.181; Maybrick, (2012), pp.127–132] when the former institution was reassigned to be used for military purposes [Maybrick, (2012), p.132]. In the end, she was released after having served just 15 years [Beadle, 2005a; Edwards, (2007), p.54]. At the date of her departure she was the only prisoner left at Aylesbury Prison who had also been a prisoner at Woking Prison [Maybrick, (2012), p.194]. However, her final release was not a special dispensation [Maybrick, (2012), p.251] but was the result of a review which was accorded to all 'life' prisoners after 20 years or somewhere between 15 and 20 years when there had been good behavior [Maybrick, (2012), p.211]. It does appear that Queen Victoria had an ill opinion of Mrs. Maybrick and, because of this, Mrs. Maybrick's release was only possible after the Queen's death on 22 January 1901. The Queen had convicted Mrs. Maybrick for immorality in her own mind and was hostile to reversing that decision [Christie, (1968), pp.224–225]. This was finally confirmed as proven fact in 1930 when George Earle Buckle published an edition of the Queen's letters [Christie, (1968), p.224].

Mrs. Maybrick was 41-years-old when she was released at 6:45 am on Monday 25 January 1904 [Christie, (1968), p.227; Maybrick, (2012), p.217]. She spent the last six months of her sentence recuperating at Home of the Community of the Epiphany in Truro, Cornwall, from which she was released on 20 July 1904 [Maybrick, (2012), pp.218–219]. About her time spent in Truro, Florence commented: "I look back upon the six months spent within those sacred walls as the most peaceful and happiest – in the true sense – of my life". After staying with her devoted mother in Rouen, France for three weeks [Maybrick, (2012), p.11, p.220], Mrs. Maybrick boarded the Red Star Line steamship Vaderland at Antwerp, Belgium bound for New York City [Christie, (1968), p.229; Maybrick, (2012), p.221] and 'the sacred soil of my [her] native land' [Maybrick, (2012), p.222]. Her name was entered on the ship's passenger list as Rose Ingraham "that I [she] might secure more quiet and privacy" [Maybrick, (2012), p.221]. The ship arrived in New York Harbour on 23 August 1904 [Christie, (1968), p.230; Maybrick, (2012), p.222].

After being an itinerant speaker about prison conditions for some years, Mrs. Maybrick passed away on 23 October 1941 [Adamson, (1993), p.6]. She never remarried. For over a decade before her death she had been living as a recluse with her cats in the rolling hills of the Connecticut countryside near Gaylordsville, South Kent [Christie, (1968), Chapter 15]. She was described by Colin Adamson in *The Evening Standard* newspaper (now renamed *The London Evening Standard*) of 22 April 1993 as having 'died penniless and in squalor in America' [Adamson, (1993), p.6]. She had befriended the local school staff and was a well-known local eccentric in the community and at the school. Mrs. Maybrick never again got to see her own children ("the children to whom I am dead" [Maybrick, (2012), p.223]), Bobo and Gladys, after they were forcibly removed from her, at the orders of Mr. Maybrick's domineering younger brother Michael [Graham and Emmas, (1999), p.125; Maybrick, (2012), p.25], in May 1889 [Maybrick, (2012), p.25, p.223 footnote]. According to Michael Maybrick, Bobo, who had been made acquainted with the anti-Florence Maybrick version of his mother's trial, "did not wish either his own or his sister's photograph to be sent to me [Florence]" in prison which up until then had been the annual practice [Maybrick, (2012), p.223 footnote]. For a family which was apparently never too far removed from tragedy, it is perhaps not surprising that Bobo was killed in a bizarre mining accident in Canada in April 1911, aged 29, when he drank a tube of cyanide believing it to be water [Christie, (1968), pp.245–6]. He left his sister Gladys a sizeable estate of £4,755 [Christie, (1968), p.246]. For her part, Gladys married in 1912 and died in South Wales in 1971 aged 85.

With very little supporting evidence Feldman (2007, pp.181–183) concludes that Florence had an illegitimate son, William Graham (Billy Graham's father/author Anne Graham's grandfather), born in Hartlepool, England in January 1879 when she was 16-years-old [see also Beadle, 2005a; Graham and Emmas, (1999), p.xxi]. Feldman (2007) surmises that this child's existence explains why Florence hoped to see 'them' (plural) [*Sunday News*, 1 May 1927, cited in Feldman, (2007), pp.181–182], meaning 'her children' (plural), in a last visit to England in 1927 when she already knew that her son Bobo had died in the 1911 mining accident and Gladys was her only other child with James [Feldman, (2007), p.183].

6: Recent developments: the 'Jack-the-Ripper' diary

The discovery of the alleged 'Jack the Ripper' diary was made in May 1991 [Beadle, 2005a; Begg, (2005), p.369; Skinner, (1999), p.x], when a Liverpudlian unemployed scrap-metal merchant Michael Barrett was allegedly handed the diary by his drinking friend the late Tony Devereux [Whitehead and Rivett, (2012), p.124], a retired printer (Knightley, 1993; Schoettler, 1993), in Liverpool pub The Saddle Inn (4) [Begg, (2005), p.369; Knightley, 1993]. The diary (hereafter referred to as 'the diary') claims internally to be authored by the 19th century Liverpool cotton merchant James Maybrick (25 October 1838–11 May 1889) [Adamson, (1993), p.6; Edwards, (2007), p.54; Gowers, (1995); Harrison, (2008), p.215; Skinner, (1999), p.x] and also to be the diary of the never apprehended Whitechapel serial-killer 'Jack the Ripper' of 1888 [Adamson, (1993), p.6; Beadle, 2005a; Edwards, (2007), p.54; Feldman, 2007; Harrison, (2008), p.215; Knightley, 1993; Linder et al., 2003; Schoettler, 1993].

Chapter 2

Noted Jack the Ripper author Keith Skinner (1999, p.ix) writes that: "the alleged 'diary of Jack the Ripper' has always been shrouded in controversy, ever since it first came into the public domain back in 1992". Before the discovery of the diary, which has somewhat dubious 'provenance' [Beadle, 2005b; Begg, (2005), p.369; George, 2006; Knightley, 1993), no writer on the Jack the Ripper murders of 1888 had ever nominated James Maybrick as a plausible suspect [Harrison, (2008), p.214; May, 2007) 5. It was the internal diary references to 'Battlecrease House', in Riversdale Road, Liverpool, which led Michael Barrett, in his follow-up private research, to conclude that the diary's author was clearly presenting himself to the world as being James Maybrick [Harrison, (2008), p.214].

Tony May (2007) from Hastings, East Sussex comments as follows: "he [Maybrick] was not connected to the enquiry at the time, and had not even been thought of as a suspect until the diary came to light so, in fairness to him, [i]f we believe the diary to be a fake I think we should all acknowledge his innocence". However, despite voluminous debate amongst Ripperologists (students of the Jack the Ripper murders) over the past 20 years and numerous forensic tests of ink, phraseology, and hand-writing, the possibility that the diary is in fact genuine has not been conclusively disproved [Edwards, (2007), p.54; George, 2007)6. Christopher T. George (2007), the Editor of Ripperologist magazine, writes as follows: "the diary has not been conclusively proven to be a hoax because no one has been proven conclusively to have forged it". The fact that forgery has not been proven [Harrison, (2008), p.230] is itself significant given that the 'Hitler diaries', for which the Sunday Times paid £1 million in 1983 (Schoettler, 1993), were exposed as fraudulent within a relatively short space of time (Knightley, 1993; Schoettler, 1993). In fact, a leading history professor has stated that the diary is 'probably genuine' or it would have been proven to be a forgery by now. Harrison (2008, p.230) observes that: "[the diary] has survived possibly the most rigorous investigation of any manuscript this [20th] century".

A more satisfactory provenance was later given the diary when Michael Barrett's ex-wife Anne Graham claimed that her late father Billy had been bequeathed the diary among the possessions of his grandmother Elizabeth Formby (Beadle, 2005a) before World War II; had first seen it when he came home on leave from the army in 1943; and had finally taken possession of it in 1950 [Begg, (2005), p.371]. Ms. Graham gave the diary to Tony Devereux, so that he would give it to her then husband Barrett. Ms. Graham was hoping that her then unemployed husband would use it to write a novel; she did not give it to him personally because she was worried he would bother her aging father with endless questions about it [Beadle, 2005a; Begg, (2005), p.372]. If this story is to be believed it points in favour of the diary's authenticity since there are facts in the diary which were not made public until 1987 (Knightley, 1993). It follows unarguably, from the internal text of the diary, that James Maybrick and Jack the Ripper are one and the same person [Harrison, (2008), p.215]. Given the fact that forgery has not been proven [Harrison, (2008), p.230], it is certainly not impossible that it is in fact a genuine document. The possible origins of the diary are as follows:

a) it is a modern forgery
b) it is an old forgery written for unknown reasons but perhaps to benefit Florence during the trial
c) it was written by James Maybrick but the events described are pure fantasy
d) James Maybrick really was Jack the Ripper.

According to the diary, Mrs. Maybrick's infidelity (the diary refers to her as 'the whore' and 'the whoring mother' [Beadle, 2005a; Graham and Emmas, (1999), p.64]) in turn led her husband James into a period of mental anguish (mixed with sexual excitement [Begg, (2005), p.370; Graham and Emmas, (1999), p.71]). This prolonged intense emotional state then led to the series of Jack the Ripper murders where the casual prostitutes of the East End of London literally stood in as 'scapegoat[s]' [Graham and Emmas, (1999), p.53] for the 'whoring' Florence.

My concluding comments about the diary are as follows: The Jack-the-Ripper diary, incriminating James Maybrick, is an interesting modern development which has not yet been conclusively proven or disproven although it is regarded as suspect by most Jack-the-Ripper scholars. If the diary's internal claim is valid, James Maybrick confessed his crimes to his wife prior to his death but this was not mentioned in court for fear that it would grant Florence an additional 'motive' for murder. However, the importance of the Florence Maybrick case today in no way stands or falls on the validity of the diary. For 100 years the Jack-the-Ripper case and the Florence Maybrick poison case were linked only by their closeness in time.

7: Conclusions

The criminal trial of Mrs. Florence Maybrick, held in Liverpool, England during the height of the British Empire 1889, is widely regarded as one of the greatest travesties of justice in British legal history where even the judge at the end of the trial remarked "well, they can't convict her on that evidence" and the chief prosecutor nodded his head in agreement. Mrs. Maybrick was tried for murdering her husband via arsenic poisoning. However, the trial became a morality trial when the presiding judge, Mr. Justice Stephen, linked Mrs. Maybrick's demonstrated adultery to her alleged desire to physically remove her husband by administering poison. Mr. Justice Stephen was wrong to attempt to, in the words of his brother Sir Leslie, turn his own criminal court into a 'school of morality'. The Jack-the-Ripper diary, incriminating James Maybrick, is an interesting modern development which has not yet been conclusively proven or disproven. However, the importance of the Florence Maybrick case today in no way stands or falls on the validity of the diary.

Szijártó (2002, p.211, emphasis added) writes that microhistory can usefully, when "contextualis[ed] as full[y] as possible, put the stress on the ramifications of the single case". The Florence Maybrick trial of 1889 remains today a timely reminder for an international audience of the fallibility and inherent weaknesses of the legal system and the desperate need to retain Courts of Criminal Appeal within the courts system. Following Szijártó (2002, p.211), "[we must] step beyond the individual case and proceed towards the general". I was lecturing in the Fiji Islands at the time this paper was written (2013–2015). It is fortunate that Fiji has a Court of Appeal enshrined in the new 2013 Constitution7 [Section 99(1)- (5), Government of Fiji, (2013), p.57].

However, I humbly suggest that there should be a splitting up of this court into a Court of Criminal Appeal and a Court of Appeal for civil (non-criminal) cases. The Maybrick case also suggests that senior judges aged over 55 years, and especially those who have suffered strokes or head injuries, need to be regularly evaluated by their peers or by other qualified persons. Mental decline can occur earlier than expected and can have devastating consequences. The Maybrick case also highlights the weakness of the English jury system where uneducated people are asked to pass judgement on what must appear to them to be complex medical evidence. Christie (1968, pp.78–79) commented that the jurors lacked "the technical training to cope with the complex medical and legal testimony". In the Florence Maybrick trial the jurors were overly impressed by the bearing, reputation, and social standing of the judge and of the star medical practitioner witness, Dr. Stevenson, who testified in a manner prejudicial to the interests of the accused.

Chapter 2

References

Adamson, C. (1993) 'Is this the face of Jack the Ripper?', 22 April, p.6, Evening Standard, UK.

Beadle, W. (2005a) Revisiting the Maybrick 'Diary' – Part One [online] http://www.jamesmaybrick.org/pdf%20files/Diary%20(William%20Beadle%20article).pdf (accessed 18 June 2013).

Beadle, W. (2005b) Revisiting the Maybrick 'Diary' – Part Two [online] http://www.jamesmaybrick.org/pdf%20files/Diary%20(William%20Beadle%20article).pdf (accessed 18 June 2013).

Begg, P. (2005) Jack the Ripper: The Definitive History, revised paperback edition, Pearson Education, Harlow.

Christie, T.L. (1968) Etched in Arsenic, Philadelphia Lippincott, Philadelphia, PA.

Edwards, M. (2007) Mind to Kill, Grange Books, Hoo, Kent.

Evans, S.P.and Skinner, K. (2000) The Ultimate Jack the Ripper Sourcebook: An Illustrated Encyclopedia, Constable and Robinson, London.

Feldman, P. (2007) Jack the Ripper: the Final Chapter, paperback edition, Virgin Books, London.

George, C.T. (2006) 'Untitled forum post', 11 August, Yoliverpool.com [online] http://www.yoliverpool.com/forum/showthread.php?2439-James-Maybrick (accessed 26 June2013).

George, C.T. (2007) 'Untitled forum post', 2 May, Yoliverpool.com [online] http://www.yoliverpool.com/forum/showthread.php?2439-James-Maybrick/page3 (accessed 26 June 2013).

Government of Fiji (2013) Constitution of the Republic of Fiji [online] http://www.paclii.org/fj/Fiji-Constitution-English-2013.pdf (accessed 24 June 2016).

Gowers, R. (1995) 'At each other's' throats over Jack the Ripper', 31 August, The Independent, UK [online] http://www.independent.co.uk/news/at-each-others-throats-over-jack-the-ripper-1598714.html (accessed 28 August 2013).

Graham, A.E. and Emmas, C. (1999) The Last Victim: The Extraordinary Life of Florence Maybrick, the Wife of Jack the Ripper, Headline Book Publishing, London.

Harrison, S. (2008) 'The diary of Jack the Ripper', in Jakubowski, M. and Braund, N. (Eds.): The Mammoth Book of Jack the Ripper, pp.213–236, American edition, Running Press Book Publishers, Philadelphia, PA.

Knightley, P. (1993) 'Is this man Jack the Ripper?: certainly a lot of money is being spent trying to tell you so', 29 August, The Independent, UK [online] http://www.independent.co.uk/news/uk/is-this-man-jack-the-ripper-certainly-a-lot-of-money-is-being-spent-trying-to-tell-you-sophillip-knightley-a-veteran-of-publishing-hoaxes-untangles-the-evidence--and-feels-he-hasbeen-here-before-1464073.html (accessed 14 June 2013).

Linder, S., Morris, C. and Skinner, K. (2003) Ripper Diary: The Inside Story, Sutton Publishing, London.

May, T. (2007) 'Untitled forum post', 2 November, Yoliverpool.com [online] http://www.yoliverpool.com/forum/showthread.php?2439-James-Maybrick/page4 (accessed 26 June 2013).

Maybrick, F. (2012) Mrs. Maybrick's Own Story: My Fifteen Lost Years, originally published 1904, Forgotten Books, New York, NY.

Morland, N. (1957) This Friendless Lady, Frederick Muller, London.

O'Brien, R.B. (1901) Life of Lord Russell of Killowen, Smith, Elder and Co., London.

Rumbelow, D. (2013) The Complete Jack the Ripper: Fully Revised and Updated, Virgin Books, London.

Schoettler, C. (1993) 'The Ripper's 'diary,' not yet published, is being slashed to pieces', 23 September, The Baltimore Sun, USA [online] http://articles.baltimoresun.com/1993-09-23/features/1993266235_1_jack-the-ripper-diary-gryphon (accessed 18 June 2013).

Skinner, K. (1999) 'Foreword', The Last Victim: The Extraordinary Life of Florence Maybrick, the Wife of Jack the Ripper, pp.ix–xv, Headline Book Publishing, London.

Stephen, J.F. (1890) A General View of the Criminal Law of England, 2nd ed., Macmillan, London and New York, NY [reproduced from the original copy held at Harvard Law School Library as part of the Gale Making of the Modern Law: Legal Treatises, 1800-1926 series).

Szijártó, I. (2002) 'Four arguments for microhistory', Rethinking History, Vol. 6, No. 2, pp.209–215.

Whitehead, M. and Rivett, M. (2012) Jack the Ripper, Pocket Essentials, Harpenden, Hertfordshire.

Notes

1 The population of Norfolk had been 21,966 in 1880, rising to 34,871 ten years later.
2 However, Morland (1957), incorrectly it seems, dates the first meeting of the couple to a trip from the USA to England in 1881 not 1880. This is why he, also incorrectly, assumes that the marriage occurred almost immediately after disembarking the ship.
3 The jury consisted of three plumbers, two farmers, one milliner, one wood-turner, one provision dealer, one grocer, one ironmonger, one house-painter, and one baker [Christie, (1968), p.79; Graham and Emmas, (1999), p.164; Maybrick, (2012), p.236 footnote].
4 This Saddle Inn (located at 86 Fountains Road) is about equidistant from Anfield and Goodison Park football stadiums and should not be confused with The Saddle Inn at 13 Dale Street (in the Liverpool city-centre).
5 I use the term 'Jack the Ripper murders' rather than the more genteel 'Whitechapel murders' not to shock but because the latter term includes all murders committed in the Whitechapel region during the period 1888–1891 which were not obviously domestics or gangland killings. These include the 'torso murders' which experts agree are unlikely to be by the same hand as the murders committed by the serial killer Jack the Ripper [Evans and Skinner, (2000), p.480; Rumbelow, (2013), p.135]. The Jack the Ripper murders are generally thought to include: Mary Ann 'Polly' Nichols, Annie Chapman; Elizabeth Stride; Catharine Eddowes and Mary Jane Kelly (all 1888); as well as possibly Martha 'Maggie' Tabram (1888); Alice MacKenzie (1889); and Frances Coles (1891).
6 For space reasons I forego in this paper any extended discussion of the debates about the diary's authenticity. Interested readers are referred to the debates for and against the diary on the Yoliverpool.com forum at: http://www.yoliverpool.com/forum/showthread.php?2439- James-Maybrick (accessed 18 June 2013).
7 This constitution was issued by the government of Frank Bainimarama in September 2013 prior to the 2014 General Election which was won by his Fiji First party.

CHAPTER 3

THE TRIAL OF FLORENCE MAYBRICK IN THE MEDIA

A COLLECTION OF PICTURES COURTESY OF ROB CLACK

POLICE · BUDGET · EDITION

EDITED · BY HAROLD FURNISS

FAMOUS CRIMES

PAST AND PRESENT

ONE · PENNY

MRS. MAYBRICK AND MR. BRIERLY AT THE LONDON HOTEL.

Vol. I.—No. 7.

ALICE YAPP SAW HER MISTRESS POURING SOMETHING FROM ONE BOTTLE INTO ANOTHER.

Vol. I.—No. 8.

"What are you doing Florence? you know that James must only take medicine from the nurses."

THE DOCTOR ANALYSED A PORTION OF ITS CONTENTS

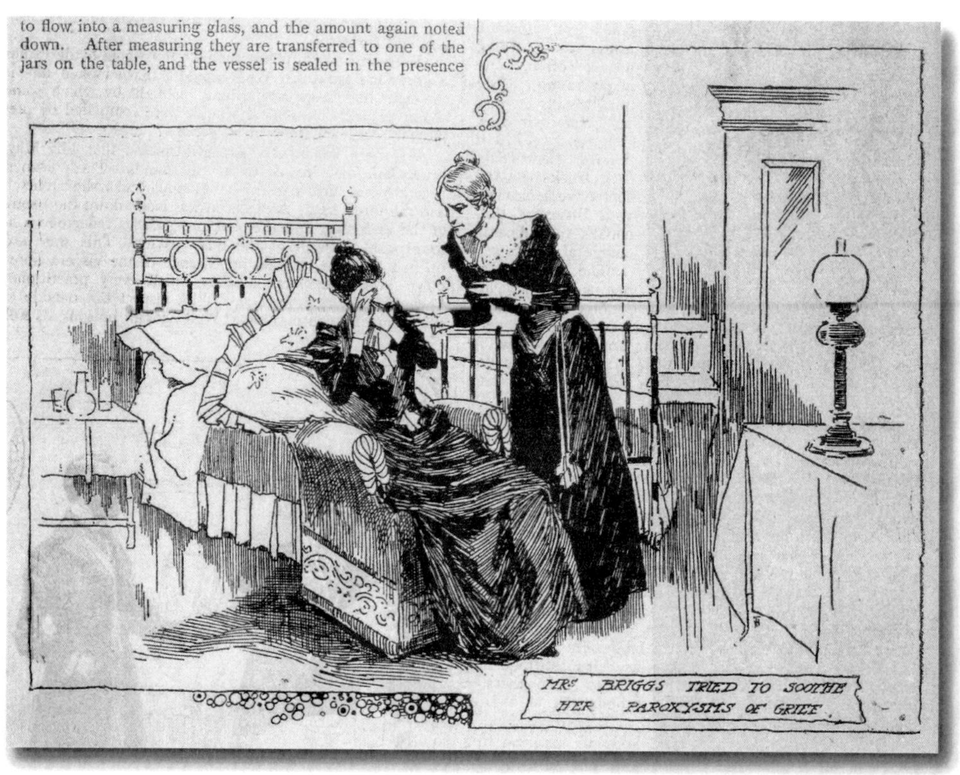
to flow into a measuring glass, and the amount again noted down. After measuring they are transferred to one of the jars on the table, and the vessel is sealed in the presence
MRS BRIGGS TRIED TO SOOTHE HER PAROXYSMS OF GRIEF.

WITNESSES IN THE LIVERPOOL POISONING CASE.
HENRY MAYBRICK
EDWIN MAYBRICK
THE COOK AT BATTLECREESE
DR DAVIS ANALYTICAL CHEMIST.
MRS BRIGGS.
MISS YAPP.
MR MICHAEL MAYBRICK.
SKETCHED IN COURT.

THE TRAGIC AND SAD STORY OF THE MAYBRICK POISONING CASE.
THE ONCE HAPPY HOME
HE IS SICK UNTO DEATH
THE FIRST QUARREL
THE CONFESSION OF INFIDELITY TO A DYING HUSBAND.
AFFECTING MEETING OF MRS MAYBRICK AND HER MOTHER IN THE CONDEMNED CELL.
THE VISIT TO A LONDON HOTEL. MRS MAYBRICKS HUSBAND'S FRIEND!
THE REMORSE THAT COMES TOO LATE

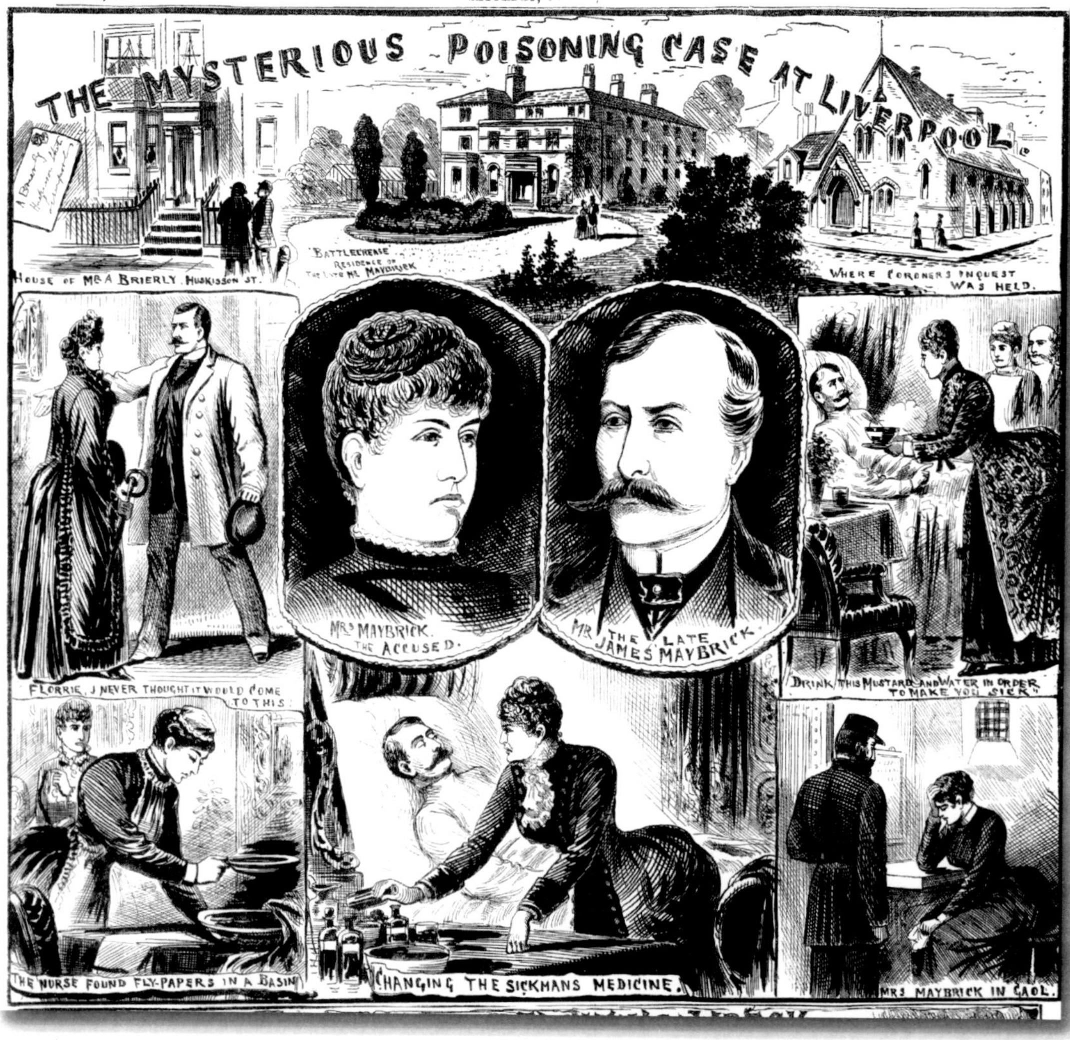
THE MYSTERIOUS POISONING CASE AT LIVERPOOL
HOUSE OF MR A BRIERLY HUSKISSON ST.
'BATTLECREASE' RESIDENCE OF THE LATE MR MAYBRICK
WHERE CORONERS INQUEST WAS HELD.
MRS MAYBRICK. THE ACCUSED.
MR THE LATE JAMES MAYBRICK
FLORRIE, I NEVER THOUGHT IT WOULD COME TO THIS:
"DRINK THIS MUSTARD AND WATER IN ORDER TO MAKE YOU SICK"
THE NURSE FOUND FLY-PAPERS IN A BASIN
CHANGING THE SICKMANS MEDICINE.
MRS MAYBRICK IN GAOL.

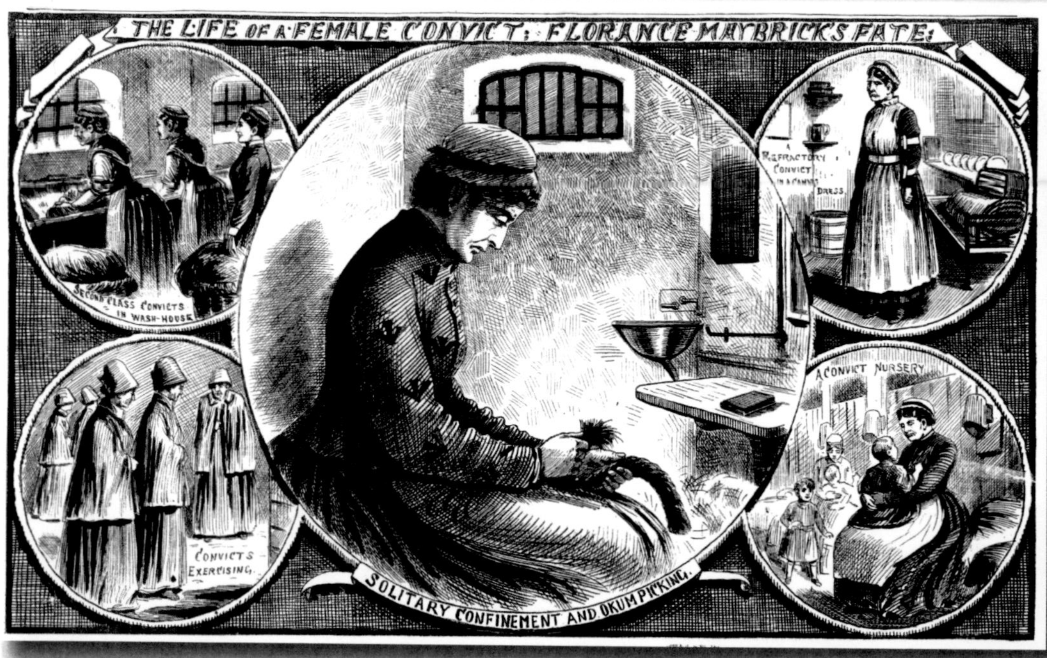

THE LIFE OF A FEMALE CONVICT: FLORANCE MAYBRICK'S FATE:
SECOND CLASS CONVICTS IN WASH-HOUSE
A REFRACTORY CONVICT IN A CANVAS DRESS
A CONVICT NURSERY
CONVICTS EXERCISING.
SOLITARY CONFINEMENT AND OKUM PICKING.

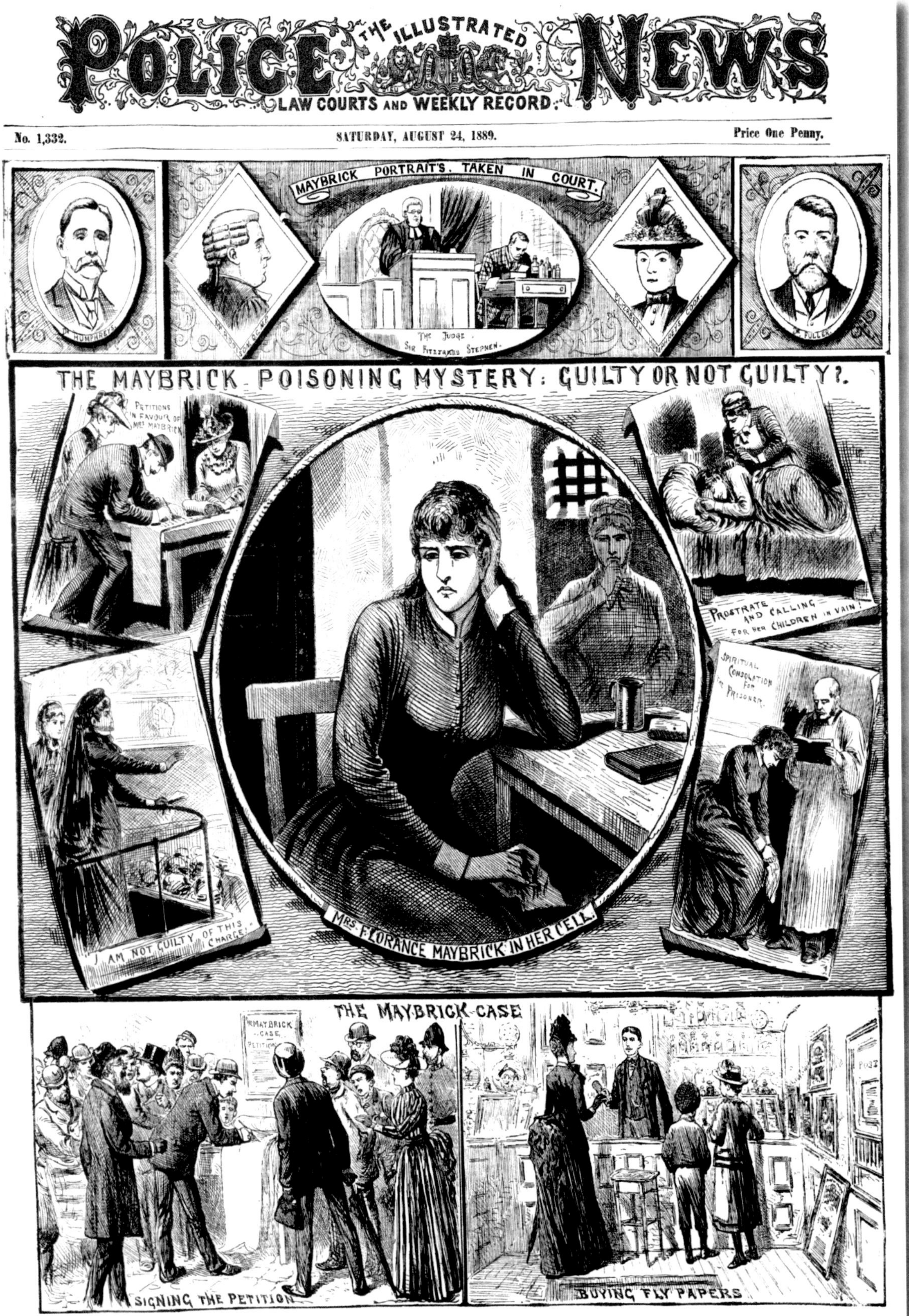

No. 1,332. SATURDAY, AUGUST 24, 1889. Price One Penny.

THE MAYBRICK POISONING MYSTERY: GUILTY OR NOT GUILTY?.

PETITIONS IN FAVOUR OF MRS MAYBRICK

PROSTRATE AND CALLING FOR HER CHILDREN IN VAIN!

SPIRITUAL CONSOLATION FOR THE PRISONER.

I AM NOT GUILTY OF THIS CHARGE!

MRS. FLORANCE MAYBRICK IN HER CELL.

THE MAYBRICK CASE

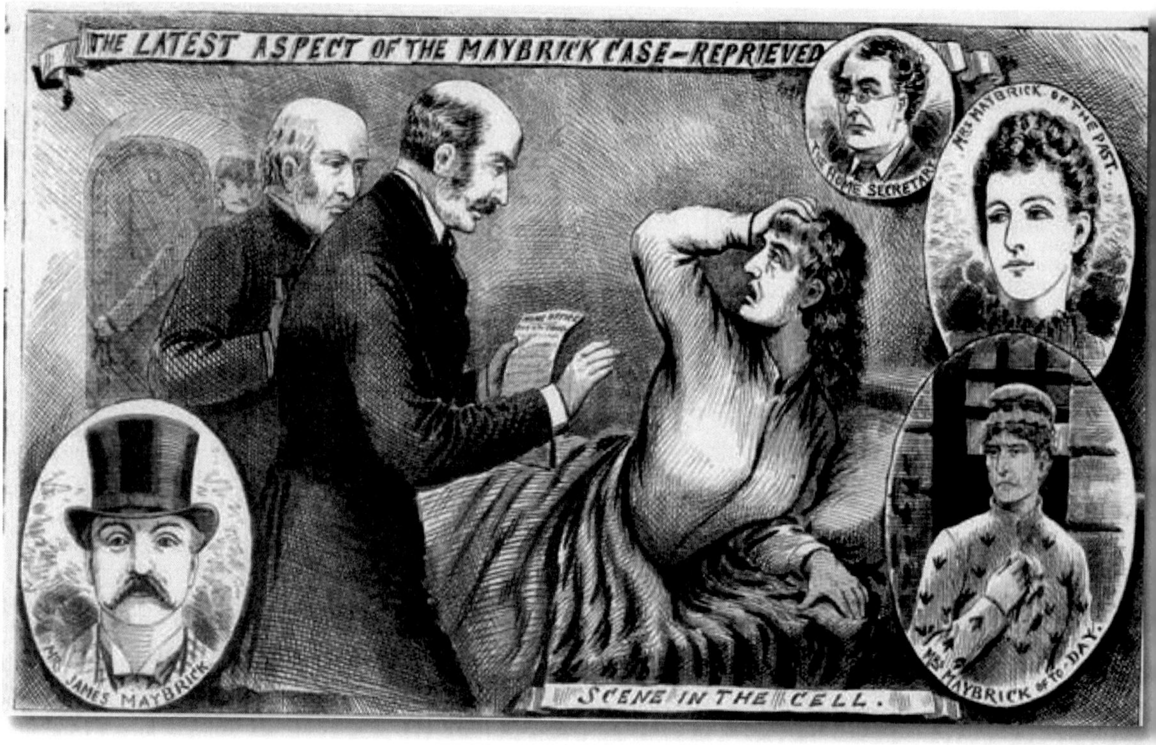

THE LATEST ASPECT OF THE MAYBRICK CASE–REPRIEVED
THE HOME SECRETARY
MRS MAYBRICK OF THE PAST.
MR. JAMES MAYBRICK
SCENE IN THE CELL.
MRS MAYBRICK OF TO-DAY.

"I SWEAR TO YOU I AM INNOCENT!"

Rev. C. H. Parkhurst, D.D., LL.D., New York: ". . . The lively interest that has been felt by Americans in the heroic experience of Mrs. Maybrick, and their profound sympathy with her in the unspeakable wrong which she seems to have suffered at the hands of the English court, will render it a great privilege to be admitted into her confidence through the medium of the written story that she is preparing to give to the public."

NOW READY

Mrs. Maybrick's Own Story

By FLORENCE ELIZABETH MAYBRICK

This famous American woman is now released after fifteen years of unjust confinement in an English prison. Stripped of her fortune, stripped of her children, Mrs. Maybrick now returns to her native America and tells her sad story, a story full of the most intense, personal interest. She has now written with her own hand a book giving for the first time her side of this awful tragedy. It is a most deeply interesting story from beginning to end. Only a fragment of this thrilling history has been told in the newspapers or magazines.

Titles of the Story's Chapters Indicating Its Absorbing Interest

The Awakening
Arrival at Walton Jail
The Trial
Under Sentence of Death
Arrival at Woking
Alone for Nine Months
The Horrors of Solitary Confinement
Hard Labor
What Dining in Prison Means
My Mother's Visits
Punishment
The Infirmary
Changed to Aylesbury
Humanizing Influences
Tragedy in Prison
A Noble Gift
Things That Might be Different
A Visit from Lord Russell of Killowen
The Officers' Mess
The Governor
The Dawn of Liberty
My Children
The Eve of Liberty
A Concluding Word

She was convicted by a judge now known to have been insane—convicted of the awful crime of poisoning her husband, an Englishman of wealth and social standing.

Within three days of the time that she was to be hanged, her sentence was commuted to penal servitude for life, beginning with nine months of solitary confinement, the privilege being denied her even of talking.

She is now released after years of appeals—urgent appeals by Presidents Cleveland, Harrison, McKinley, and Roosevelt, and from Secretaries Blaine, Olney, and Hay. And after the most solemn declaration of her innocence by Lord Chief Justice Russell, head of all the Courts of England.

FLORENCE MAYBRICK.

A more awful wrong can scarcely be imagined than that done this woman.

She appeals from English injustice to the American sense of justice and fair play.

And now writes out in full her side of the wrong done her, and asks for vindication in the minds of all Americans.

"Mrs. Maybrick's Own Story" of her trial, of what preceded her trial, her family life, and her fifteen years' experience in prison, make a book of thrilling interest.

It is an eloquent appeal. It contains not one word of bitterness. At times we hear the agonizing cry of a mother who is denied even a sight of her babes, of the innocence of womanhood outraged beyond endurance. Is there a single American, woman or man, who will not grant her a hearing and help to make known her side of this terrible tragedy!

Rev. John White Chadwick, Pastor Second Unitarian Society of Brooklyn: "The attention paid to Mrs. Maybrick's book should be as wide as the interest excited by her case. Those who have all along had perfect faith in her will wish to hear her speaking in her own voice, and those who have doubted or denied her innocence are in honor bound to read what she has written. Believing her to have been shamefully wronged, I trust that the reception accorded to her book will fill her purse and comfort her sad heart."

12mo, Cloth, 400 Pages, 16 Half-Tone Illustrations. Price, $1.20, net; by Mail, $1.30. Subscription Edition, handsomely bound, wide margins, photogravure portrait of Mrs. Maybrick. Each copy signed separately by her with her own hand; Price, $2.00, postage free. AGENTS WANTED

FUNK & WAGNALLS COMPANY, Publishers, New York and London

CHAPTER 4

A SCRAPBOOK FROM HELL? THE WHISTLE STOP TOUR OF THE DIARY OF JACK THE RIPPER

BY RICHARD C. COBB

The Diary at the York Jack The Ripper Conference 2012
"Original diary manuscript Copyright © Robert Smith, 1993"

What would it take to convince you of someone being Jack the Ripper? How about a signed and detailed confession? That's exactly what the world was presented with, on Monday 9th March 1992, but was there more to the Diary of Jack the Ripper than met the eye?

On Monday, 13th April 1992, Mike Barrett, a former scrap metal dealer from Liverpool, in his late forties, walked into the offices of Rupert Crew Ltd, a London literary agency. Barrett produced a scuffed, black-and-gilt leather-bound volume containing 64 or 65 pages (accounts differ) handwritten in ink, and signed 'Jack the Ripper'. Barrett said he had been given the diary at The Saddle Inn; a traditional public house on the Fountains Road, Anfield, by a drinking friend, Tony Devereux. Devereux, a former printer on the Liverpool Post, died eight months earlier, on Thursday 8th August 1991, so his story could not be confirmed, but his family insisted that had he never mentioned the diary to them. Mike Barrett telephoned 'Pan Books' and was told to get an agent. He wondered whether Rupert Crew could handle the diary and how much would it be worth?

The agency had among its clients, author Shirley Harrison, who said she had been considering writing a book about the infamous Florence Maybrick murder trial of 1889. On the surface, the trial of Florence Maybrick would have little to do with the events in Whitechapel the previous Autumn. But there was no doubt that the diary pointed a firm finger to Florence's husband James as being the author of the Diary.

Chapter 4

The Diary was not signed or named, but there were enough details for it to be obviously written about James Maybrick. Clues mentioned within the pages of the diary included a mention of Maybrick's home, known as Battlecrease. Suddenly, the agency had on its hands not only a diary revealing the Jack The Ripper's inner-most thoughts, but also - at last - the true identity of the Ripper.

Parts of the diary are emotional and graphic. The writer confesses: *Oh, what deeds shall I commit. For how could one suspect that I could be capable of such things.' There are hints of cannibalism: 'I will boil it and eat it with freshly pickled carrots.'* ("Original diary manuscript Copyright © Robert Smith, 1993")

He concludes by saying that he will leave the diary in a place where it will be found, and signs off: *I do give my name that all know of me, so history do tell, what love can do to a gentle man born. Yours truly, Jack the Ripper.'* ("Original diary manuscript Copyright © Robert Smith, 1993")

If Maybrick was indeed the Ripper - and he is known to have frequented brothels - one aspect of the mystery is immediately explained. The murders lasted only three months and ceased abruptly in November 1888. The explanation is one that the police never considered at the time: that Jack the Ripper was himself murdered, poisoned with arsenic by his American wife, Florence, who was having an affair with another cotton broker.

To some the uncertain provenance of the diary was enough to convince them that it had to be a hoax, in fact you would struggle to find anyone in the early days who took the diary seriously, and rightly so. Only a few years before, the Hitler diaries caused a lot of damage and people didn't want their reputation tarnished again by something that most considered, at the time, a hoax. As time went on however, proving it a forgery became more and more difficult and soon the theory was gaining support. Some took the view that further research seemed to support the journals claims, not diminish them.

Supporters of the dairy say that historical research, image enhancement, laser technology and extensive analysis of ink, paper and handwriting, have shown beyond all reasonable doubt that this document was written at the time of the Whitechapel murders by the man responsible. Seven experts, including a forensic scientist, a handwriting analyst, a psychiatrist and a criminologist agreed with this. The Diary itself was shown to be Victorian and the ink was supposedly shown to be from around 1921 give or take 12 years. This presents an interesting problem as details contained inside the Journal didn't become available to the public until 1987. Was it possible that we were stepping inside the mind of the real Jack the Ripper for the very first time?

It's true to say even those who claim the diary is a fake would tell you that there was information contained within its pages that at least showed the authors attention to detail. So what motive would James Maybrick have for becoming Jack the Ripper? In the diary, the author makes the claim that he had seen his wife - whom he calls "the bitch," or "the whore" in the pages of the diary - with her unnamed lover in the Whitechapel district of Liverpool. The subsequent rage that he experienced following this sighting sent him on a murderous rampage in the Whitechapel district of London, in the course of which he mutilated and killed five prostitutes. This may not be the most plausible explanation for someone to go on a killing spree, but having studied serial killers for over 25 years I have certainly heard of stranger motives. The journal contains a long description of the murders before ending with the assertion "I give my name that all know of me, so history do tell, what love can do to a gentle man born. Yours truly, Jack the Ripper." ("Original diary manuscript Copyright © Robert Smith, 1993")

Up until the emergence of the diary there had never been any suggestion that James Maybrick may have been Jack the Ripper and the only real evidence against him as a suspect is his own supposed confession in the pages of his diary. So, is it possible a would-be forger, could find a subject that would fit all the requirements of a plausible suspect? This is where normally a hoax would be discovered, as researchers go into the fine details of the subject matter, but it seems all research that has been carried out on James Maybrick, has not been able to dismiss him as a suspect. However at the same time it has also not been able to pin him down as being the Whitechapel murderer either. So his viability as a Jack the Ripper suspect comes down to whether or not he wrote the diary and, if he did, does the content of the Diary correspond with the known facts.

The diary itself is a Victorian scrapbook or photo album, with twenty pages torn out of the front. The paper and ink have defied conclusive scientific analysis – while some reports claim the diary is an obvious fake, others have stated it is old. Some tests have found the type of ink used consistent with the Late Victorian Period, others claim it is too modern. Some experts have claimed the ink has faded or bronzed over the last 20 years, others that it has remained the same. One of the biggest problems is the diary's provenance. It stops short at Tony Devereux and raises the question: where has the diary been all these years? The present owner of Maybrick's mansion, Battlecrease House, is Paul Dodd, a schoolteacher. He revealed that the house was extensively re-wired in the early 1990's. Could the electricians have found the diary when lifting the floorboards? They have vigorously denied having done so. Yet some did admit to drinking in the same public house as Mike Barrett and Tony Devereux.

Another puzzling aspect of the Diary involves an entry where the writer says that he confessed all to his wife. If this had been true it would have been logical for Florence to have used this knowledge as part of her defence at her sensational trial in July 1889, where she stood accused of poisoning her husband. She could have easily claimed she had feared for her own life, after her husband had confessed to her that he was Jack the Ripper, but she did not. Nor did she mention it when she was released 15 years later, when returned to the United States and wrote her memoirs. Even in those days a book entitled 'I Was Jack the Ripper's Wife' would have had an enormous sale.

Another problem with the Diary, is that it could be interpreted as hinting that the author has written two famous letters which appeared during the Jack the Ripper murders. The two letters in question are known as "The Dear Boss" letter and the "From Hell" letter.

The Dear Boss letter was received by the Central news agency on September 27th, 1888, this letter was originally believed to be just another hoax. Three days later, the double murder of Elizabeth Stride and Catherine Eddowes made them reconsider, especially once they learned a portion of the latter's earlobe was found cut off from the body, eerily reminiscent of a promise made within the letter.

The letter read:

Dear Boss Envelope

Dear Boss,

I keep on hearing the police have caught me but they wont fix me just yet. I have laughed when they look so clever and talk about being on the right track. that joke about Leather Apron gave me real fits. I am down on whores and I shant quit ripping them till I do get buckled. Grand work the last job was. I gave the lady no time to squeal. How can they catch me now. I love my work and want to start again. You will soon hear of me with my funny little games. I saved some of the proper red stuff in a ginger beer bottle over the last job to write with but it went thick like glue and I cant use it. Red ink is fit enough I hope ha. ha. The next job I do I shall clip the ladys ears off and send to the police officers just for jolly wouldn't you. Keep this letter back till I do a bit more work, then give it out straight. My knife's so nice and sharp I want to get to work right away if I get a chance. Good Luck. Yours truly

Jack the Ripper

Dont mind me giving the trade name

PS Wasnt good enough to post this before I got all the red ink off my hands curse it No luck yet. They say I'm a doctor now. ha ha

Whether or not the letter was a hoax, it is the first written reference, which we know of, that uses the name "Jack the Ripper" in reference to the Whitechapel murderer. The author of the diary however, over uses the words *"Ha! Ha!"* throughout the Journal. Almost as if they are purposefully trying to link themselves to this infamous letter to give the diary more weight.

Chapter 4

Front and Reverse of Dear Boss Letter

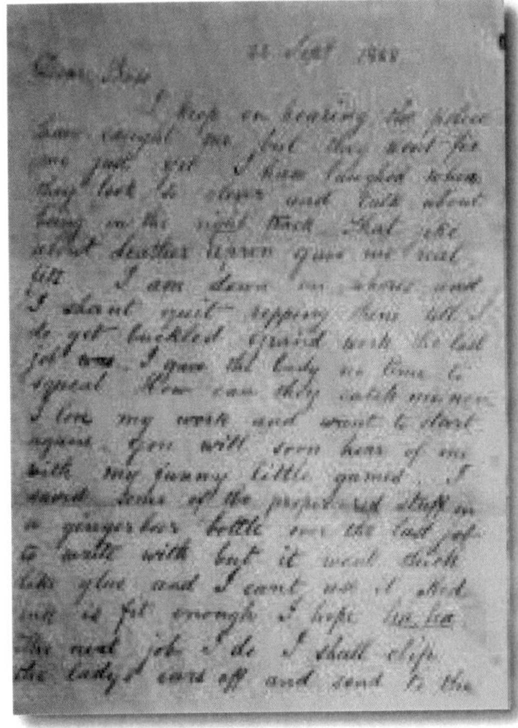

25 Sept 1888

Dear Boss

I keep on hearing the police have caught me but they wont fix me just yet. I have laughed when they look so clever and talk about being on the right track. That joke about Leather Apron gave me real fits. I am down on whores and I shant quit ripping them till I do get buckled. Grand work the last job was. I gave the lady no time to squeal. How can they catch me now. I love my work and want to start again. You will soon hear of me with my funny little games. I saved some of the proper red stuff in a ginger beer bottle over the last job to write with but it went thick like glue and I cant use it. Red ink is fit enough I hope ha. ha. The next job I do I shall clip the ladys ears off and send to the

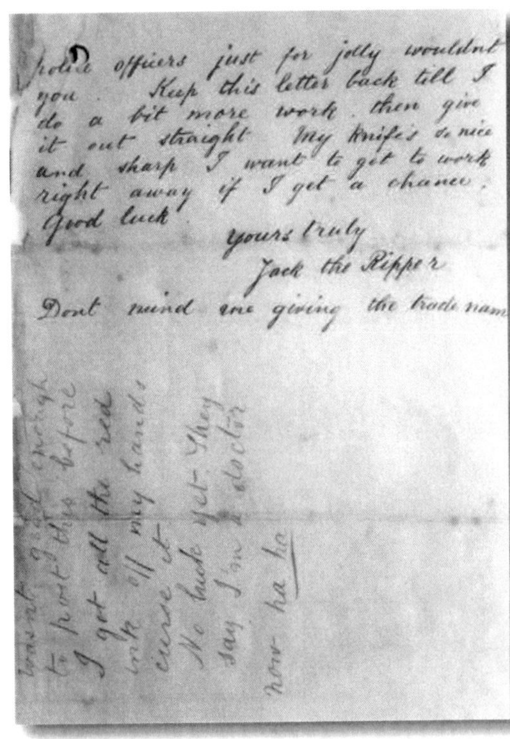

police officers just for jolly wouldnt you. Keep this letter back till I do a bit more work, then give it out straight. My knifes so nice and sharp I want to get to work right away if I get a chance. Good luck.

yours truly

Jack the Ripper

Dont mind me giving the trade name

wasnt good enough to post this before I got all the red ink off my hands curse it. No luck yet. They say I'm a doctor now. ha ha

In another section of the diary the writer goes on to say he had taken parts of the body away with him and he intended to *"fry and eat it".* This is almost certainly a direct reference to the *"From Hell"* letter.

On October 16th 1888, George Lusk, the president of the Whitechapel Vigilance Committee, received a three-inch-square cardboard box in his mail. Inside was half a human kidney preserved in wine, along with the following letter. Medical reports carried out by Dr. Openshaw found the kidney to be very similar to the one removed from Catherine Eddowes, though his findings were inconclusive either way. The letter read as follows:

From hell.
Mr Lusk,

Sor
I send you half the Kidne I took from one
woman and prasarved
it for you tother piece I fried and ate it was
very nise.
I may send you the bloody knif that took it out if
you only wate a whil longer
signed

Catch me when you can Mishter Lusk

The problem with claiming or hinting that the author wrote both letters is that it's quite clear that both are written by two different hands and neither of them are in the handwriting of the Diary. This aspect of the journal has never been fully explained.

Then we have Mike Barrett (the man who claimed to have been given the diary) and his wife Anne. Anne would later claim that the diary came from her family and that she had arranged for it to be given to Barrett in the hope he would write a book about it. Barrett then threw in a bombshell, he changed his story and said that he actually forged the book, assisted by his wife. His confession read;

Michael Barrett's Confessions
January 5 1995
From a sworn affidavit:

I MICHAEL BARRETT, make oath and state as follows:-

That I am an Author by occupation and a former Scrap Metal Merchant. I reside alone at XXXXXXXXXXXXXXXXX, and at this time I am incapacitated due to an accident., for which I am attending Hospital as an out-patient. I have this day been informed that it may be neccessary (sic) for them to amputate two of the fingers on my right hand.

Since December 1993 I have been trying, through the press, the Publishers, the Author of the Book, Mrs Harrison, and my Agent Doreen Montgomery to expose the fraud of ' The Diary of Jack the Ripper ' ("the diary").

Nobody will believe me and in fact some very influential people in the Publishing and Film world have been doing everything to discredit me and in fact they have gone so far as to introduce a new and complete story of the original facts of the Diary and how it came to light.

The facts of this matter are outlined as follows: -

I Michael Barratt (sic) was the author of the original diary of 'Jack the Ripper' and my wife, Anne Barrett, hand wrote it from my typed notes and on occasions at my dictation, the details of which I will explain in due course.
The idea of the Diary came from discussion between Tony Devereux, Anne Barrett my wife and myself, there came I time when I believed such a hoax was a distinct possibility. We looked closely at the background of James Maybrick and I read everything to do with the Jack the Ripper matter. I felt Maybrick was an ideal candidate for Jack the Ripper. Most important of all, he could not defend himself. He was not 'Jack the Ripper' of that I am certain, but, times, places, visits to London and all that fitted. It was to (sic) easey (sic).

I told my wife Anne Barrett, I said, "Anne I'll write a best seller here, we can't fail".

Once I realised we could do it. We had to find the necessary materials, paper, pens and ink. I gave this serious consideration.

Roughly round about January, February 1990 Anne Barrett and I finally decided to go ahead and write the Diary of Jack the Ripper. In fact Anne purchased a Diary, a red leather backed Diary for L25.00p, she made the purchase through a firm in the 1986 Writers Year Book, I cannot remember their name, she paid for the Diary by cheque in the amount of L25 which was drawn on her Lloyds Bank Account, Water Street Branch, Liverpool. When this Diary arrived in teh post I decided it was of no use, it was very small. My wife is now in possession of this Diary in fact she asked for it specifically recently when I saw her at her home address XXXXXXXXXXXXXXX

At about the same time as all this was being discussed by my wife and I. I spoke to William Graham about our idea. This was my wifes father and he said to me, its a good idea, if you can get away with it and in fact he gave me L50 towards expences which I expected to pay at least for the appropriate paper should I find it.

I feel sure it was the end of January 1990 when I went to the Auctioneer, Outhwaite & Litherland.

Chapter 4

It was about 11.30am in the morning when I attended the Auctioneers. I found a photograph Album which contained approximately (sic) 125 pages of phootgraphs. They were old photographs and they were all to do with the 1914/1918 1st World War. This Album was part of lot No.126 which was for auction with a 'brass compass,' it looked to me like a 'seaman's Compass,' it was round faced with a square encasement, all of which was brass, it was marked on the face, North South, East and West in heavy lettering. I particularly noticed that the compass had no 'fingers.'

When the bidding stated (sic) I noticed another man who was interested in the items (sic) he was smartly dressed, I would say in his middle forties, he was interested in the photographs. I noticed that his collar and tie were immaculate and I think he was a Military man.

This man bid up to 45 and then I bid 50 and the other man dropped out.

At this stage I was given a ticket on which was marked the item number and the price I had bid. I then had to hand this ticket over to the Office and I paid 50. This ticked was stamped. I woman, slim build, aged about 35/40 years dealt with me and she asked me my name, which I gave as P Williams. I think I gave the number as 47. When I was asked for details about me the name Williams arose because I purchased my house from a Mr P Williams, the road name I used is in fact the next street to my mums address.

I then returned to the Auction Room with my stamped ticket and handed it over to an assistant, a young man, who gave me the Lot I had purchased.

I was then told to return (sic) my ticket to the Office, but I did not do this and left with the Photograph Album and Compass.

When I got the Album and Compass home, I examined it closely, inside the front cover I noticed a makers stamp mark, dated 1908 or 1909 to remove this without trace I soaked the whole of the front cover in Linseed Oil, once the oil was absorbed by the front cover, which took about 2 days to dry out. I even used the heat from the gas oven to assist in the drying out.
I then removed the makers seal which was ready to fall off. I then took a 'Stanley Knife' and removed all the photographs, and quite a few pages.
I then made a mark 'kidney' shaped, just below centre inside the cover with the Knife.

This last 64 pages inside the Album which Anne and I decided would be the Diary. Anne and I went to town in Liverpool and in Bold Street I bought three pens, that would hold fountain nibs, the little brass nibs. I bought 22 brass nibs at about 7p to 12p, a variety of small brass nibs, all from the 'Medice' art gallery.

This all happened late January 1990 and on the same day that Anne and I bought the nibs we then decided to purchase the ink elsewhere and we decided to make our way to the Bluecoat Chambers, in fact we had a drink in the Empire Pub in Hanover Street on the way.
Anne Barrett and I visited the Bluecoat Chambers Art shop and we purchased a small bottle of Diamine Manuscript ink. I cannot remember the exact price of the Ink. I think it was less than a pound.

We were now ready to go and start the Diary. We went home and on the same evening that we had purchased everything, that is the materials we needed, We decided to have a practise run and we used A4 paper for this, and at first we tried it in my handwriting, but we realised and I must emphasie (sic) this, my handwriting was to (sic) disstinctive (sic) so it had to be in Anne's handwriting, after the practise run which took us approximately two days, we decided to go for hell or bust.

I sat in the living room by the rear lounge window in the corner with my word processor, Anne Barrett sat with her back on to me as she wrote the manuscript. This pose was later filmed by Paul Feldman of MIA Productions Limited.

Several days prior to our purchase of materials I had started to roughly outline the Diary on my word processor.

Anne and I started to write the Diary in all it took us 11 days. I worked on the story and then I dictated it to Anne who wrote it down in the Photograph Album and thus we produced the Diary of Jack the Ripper. Much to my regret there was a witness to this, my young daughter Caroline.

During this period when we were writing the Diary, Tony Devereux was house-bound, very ill and in fact after we completed the Diary we left it for a while with Tony being severly (sic) ill and in fact he died late May early June 1990.

During the writing of the diary of Jack the Ripper, when I was dictating to Anne, mistakes occurred from time to time for example, Page 6 of the diary, 2nd paragraph, line 9 starts with an ink blot, this blot covers a mistake when I told Anne to write down James instead of thomas. The mistake was covered by the Ink Blot.

Page 226 of the Book, page 20, centre page inverted commas, quote "TURN ROUND THREE TIMES, AND CATCH WHOM YOU MAY". This was from Punch Magazine, 3rd week in September 1888. The journalist was P.W. WENN.

Page 228 of the book, page 22 Diary, centre top verse large ink blot which covers the letter 's' which Anne Barrett wrote down by mistake.

Page 250 book, page 44 Diary, centre page, quote: "OH COSTLY INTERCOURSE OF DEATH". This quotation I took from SPHERE HISTORY OF LITERATURE, Volume 2 English Poetry and Prose 1540-1671, Ediated by Christopher Ricks, however, Anne Barrett made a mistake when she wrote it down, she should have written down 'O' not 'OH'.

Page 184 in Volume 2 referrs (sic).
When I disposed of the photographs from the Album by giving them to William Graham, I kept one back. This photograph was of a Grave, with a Donkey standing nearby. I had actualy written the "Jack the Ripper Diary" first on my word processor, which I purchased in 1985, from Dixons in Church Street, Liverpool City Centre. The Diary was on two hard back discs when I had finished it. The Discs, the one Photograph, the compass, all pens and the remainder of the ink was taken by my sister Lynn Richardson to her home address, XXXXXXXXXXXXXXX. When I asked her at a later date for the property she informed me that after an article had appeared in the Daily Post, by Harold Brough, she had destroyed everything, in order to protect me.

When I eventually did the deal with Robert Smith he took possession of the Diary and it went right out of my control. There is little doubt in my mind that I have been hoodwinked or if you like conned myself. My inexperience in the Publishing game has been my downfall, whilst all around me are making money, it seems that I am left out of matters, and my Solicitors are now engaged in litigation.

I finally decided in November 1993 that enough was enough and I made it clear from that time on that the Diary of Jack the Ripper was a forgery, this brought a storm down on me, abuse and threats followed and attacks on my character as Paul Feldman led this attack, because I suppose he had the most to gain from discrediting me.

Mr. Feldman became so obsessed with my efforts to bare the truth of the matter, that he started to threaten me, he took conttrol (sic) of my wife who left me and my child and he rang me up continuously threatening and bullying me and telling me I would never see my family again. On one occasion people were banging on my windows as Feldman threatened my life over the phone. I became so frightened that I sort (sic) the help of a Private Detective Alan Gray and complaints were made to the Police which I understand are still being pursued.

Chapter 4

PUNCH, OR THE LONDON CHARIVARI.—SEPTEMBER 22, 1888.

BLIND-MAN'S BUFF.

(As played by the Police.)

"TURN ROUND THREE TIMES,
AND CATCH WHOM YOU MAY!"

It was about 1st week in December 1994 that my wife Anne Barrett visited me, she asked me to keep my mouth shut and that if I did so I could receive a payment of L20,000 before the end of the month. She was all over me and we even made love, it was all very odd because just as quickley (sic) as she made love to me she threatened me and returned to her old self. She insisted Mr Feldman was a very nice Jewish man who was only trying to help her. My wife was clearly under the influence of this man Feldman who I understand had just become separated from his own wife. It seemed very odd to me that my wife who had been hidden in London for long enough by Feldman should suddenly re-appear and work on me for Mr Feldman.

I have now decided to make this affidavit to make the situation clear with regard to the Forgery of the Jack the Ripper Diary, which Anne Barrett and I did in case anything happenes (sic) to me. I would hate to leave at this stage the name of Mr. Maybrick as a tarnished serial killer when as far as I know, he was not a killer.

I am the author of the Manuscript written by my wife Anne Barrett at my dictation which is known as The Jack the Ripper Diary.

I give my name so history do tell what love can do to a gentleman born, Yours Truly -- Michael Barrett.

Sworn at Liverpool in the
County of Merseyside, this
5th day of January 1995.

(Signed)

Before me: (Signed)

A Solicitor Empowered to Administer Oaths

D.P. HARDY & CO.,
Imperial Chambers,
XXXXXXXXXXXXXX
XXXXXXXXXXXXXX

Now normally with a detailed confession like this, that would be the end of the matter, however nothing is ever so straight forward in this bizarre case. Mike Barrett later withdrew this confession, and then subsequently withdrew the withdrawal and so on and so on, (a pattern that he has frequently repeated in the years since). Despite outlandish claims that he had faked it, he provided no proof or samples to back up his claims. At the time of writing no evidence of how they might have forged the document have been given, despite the fact a simple handwriting example would prove it beyond all doubt. So just as it looked like we had taken one step forward, we ended up taking two back. We had a journal which couldn't be proved genuine or a hoax. Surely, we couldn't see anything more puzzling or frustrating could we? Well, the big twist came in 1993 when a further piece of "evidence" surfaced that presented Maybrick as the Ripper. Something nobody was expecting.

A college caretaker, names Albert Johnson, came forward with a gold pocket watch. He had spotted the piece, dated 1846, in a Liverpool jeweller's window and paid £225 for it on Tuesday 14th July 1992. He took it home and put it in a drawer, intending to pass on to his granddaughter Daisy at a later date. Months later and whilst at work the conversation turned to watches and he informed his colleagues that he owned an 18ct Gold watch and he would bring it in to show them. When he brought it in and showed how to open the front and back, the light from the window caught the watch and showed up several scratches imbedded in the back cover. Out of curiosity he went to examine to scratches and when analysed under a microscope revealed the signature "J. Maybrick", the words "I am Jack" and the initials of the five canonical victims. Of course, right away many experts were quick to dismiss this as a hoax and a simple case of someone "jumping on the band waggon", yet strangely enough, when scientifically examined, the Watch seemed to hold up to much more scrutiny than the diary.

Dr Stephen Turgoose examined the scratches using an electron microscope in 1993 and reported the following:

Chapter 4

On the basis of the evidence…especially the order in which the markings were made, it is clear that the engravings pre-date the vast majority of superficial surface scratch marks…the wear apparent on the engravings, evidenced by the rounded edges of the markings and 'polishing out' in places, would indicate a substantial age…whilst there is no evidence which would indicate a recent (last few years) origin…it must be emphasised that there are no features observed which conclusively prove the age of the engravings. They could have been produced recently, and deliberately artificially aged by polishing, but this would have been a complex multi-stage process…many of the features are only resolved by the scanning electron microscope, not being readily apparent in optical microscopy, and so, if they were of recent origin, the engraver would have to be aware of the potential evidence available from this technique, indicating a considerable skill and scientific awareness."

The following year they were also examined by Dr Robert Wild using an electron microscope and Auger electron spectroscopy:

"Provided the watch has remained in a normal environment, it would seem likely that the engravings were at least several tens of years' age…in my opinion it is unlikely that anyone would have sufficient expertise to implant aged, brass particles into the base of the engravings."

So, now we have a Diary that defies scientific analysis (with experts unable to agree on the age of ink and when it was applied to paper) and a watch that seems to have been engraved "several tens of years" ago. If the scientific tests are to be believed the watch is genuine, but where did it come from? How did it manage to turn up the same time as the Maybrick Diary? Were they both taken from Maybricks home at the same time, perhaps during renovations to the property? Regardless of the many questions, the findings delighted the watch's owner, Albert Johnson who had paid for the tests to be done. He later said:

"We could go on for forever getting the watch tested but it wouldn't make any difference to some people…. in my own mind, I have no doubt who the Ripper was."

The book, the Diary of Jack the Ripper by Shirley Harrison was finally released in 1993. Harrison and the books publisher (and current owner of the Diary) Robert Smith, both believe the Diary to be genuine and that Maybrick was the Ripper. The waters were muddied however by the arrival on the scene of Paul Feldman, (referred to in Mike Barrett's confession) who bought the right to produce a documentary on the topic. Feldman produced his own book "The Final Chapter" in 1997, and became obsessed with proving Maybrick as author of the Diary and the Ripper. Feldman believed that Ann Graham and Albert Johnson were both descended from the Maybrick family, but no one has been able to prove this theory.

In 1998 more than 100 delegates at the International Investigative Psychology Conference at Liverpool University failed to reach a consensus on whether Jack the Ripper was in fact a Liverpool cotton trader called James Maybrick. Psychologists and police officers from as far afield as South Africa and Japan met at the conference in an attempt to decide once and for all whether or not the Maybrick diary is a forgery. The only conclusion they did reach was that the document was written by someone with a "disturbed mind" and it was therefore "fascinating", even if it was not genuine. Author Shirley Harrison, who wrote the academic work The Diary of Jack the Ripper, said: "Although I have not been able to prove that it is genuine, I seriously believe the diary deserves serious historical and academic consideration."

She said tests have failed to conclusively date the ink in which the diary was written to the 1880s, but neither could they demonstrate that the ink is not Victorian. Head of the Liverpool University Centre for Investigative Psychology, Professor David Canter, who hosted the conference, said psychological profiling shows it is "plausible" that the diary may have been written by Jack the Ripper. He said:

"The way it's written - the style of thinking - does reveal some components that are remarkably subtle. This was either produced by a very skilled author or someone with detailed knowledge of the Ripper history, or someone with enormous insight into carrying out these crimes and the person most likely to have that is the person who did carry out those crimes."

The Diary Of Jack The Ripper: Research & Conclusion

The existence of the Diary has certainly divided Ripperology. During the late 1990's and early 2000's thousands of characters of text were exchanged in debate, argument and sometimes even insults on the Casebook message board. Some felt that the Diary was genuine and James Maybrick was Jack the Ripper, others that it was a modern forgery, still a third group believed that it was a very old forgery (some believing that this didn't mean that Maybrick wasn't the Ripper or that perhaps he wrote it and was delusional). Even today the subject is controversial, and it seems that we are no nearer to figuring out just where and when it came from, or who wrote it and why.

As we come to a look at the twenty-five-year debate, two further events are worth mentioning. The first being, that at the Trial of James Maybrick held in Liverpool in 2007, respected Ripper researcher Keith Skinner was asked if he felt Maybrick was a credible Ripper suspect. His answer shocked the audience when he replied that the Diary was the subject of ongoing enquiries but "if I went into a court of law with the documents in my possession, I think the jury would reach a verdict and say, "yes, this Diary came out of Battlecrease House." (Battlecrease being James Maybrick house). He has since clarified that he did not suggest the Diary was genuine or that Maybrick was the Ripper, but beyond that has not revealed the research he possess, possibly because of contractual obligations. The second was at the 2012 Jack the Ripper Conference in York where Robert Anderson (a self-confessed Maybrickian) presented an analysis of the scientific evidence for and against the Diary. As part of the presentation, Robert Smith had brought the Diary for delegates to look at and they revealed that Smith and his solicitor travelled to Liverpool to meet with workmen who had renovated Battlecrease House. It is claimed they signed a sworn affidavit that one of their colleagues had removed from the building an old book and a woman's gold ring. This confirmed speculation of many years that builders or electricians had discovered and taken the book when working in the house.

So, it's time for speculation. Is it possible that up to three strange items were discovered during building work carried out at the Maybrick Family home in the early 1990's? Where those items removed by curious workmen? Where those items, an old leather-bound journal with handwritten notes, a gold ring and possibly a gold pocket watch? If it is possible, then ask yourself this, at some point these items were separated, the Gold watch ending up in a jeweller's shop, the journal worked its way to Mike Barrett and somewhere out there is one gold ring, but where?

CHAPTER 5

MIKE BARRETT'S RESEARCH NOTES

DONATED BY KEITH SKINNER

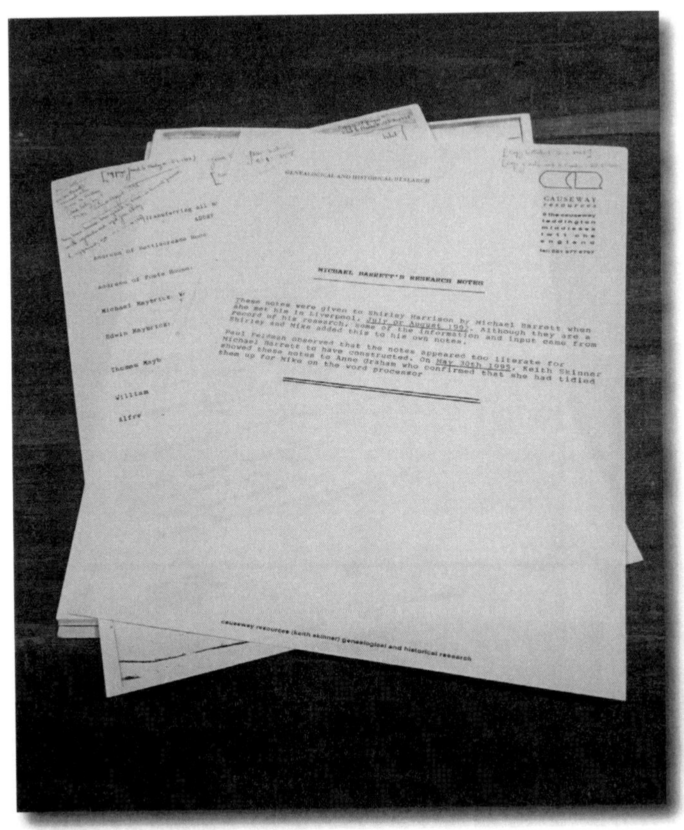

GENEALOGICAL AND HISTORICAL RESEARCH

CAUSEWAY
resources

8 the causeway
teddington
middlesex
tw11 0he
england

tel: 081 977 8797

MICHAEL BARRETT'S RESEARCH NOTES

These notes were given to Shirley Harrison by Michael Barrett when she met him in Liverpool, July or August 1992. Although they are a record of his research, some of the information and input came from Shirley and Mike added this to his own notes.

Paul Feldman observed that the notes appeared too literate for Michael Barrett to have constructed. On May 30th 1995, Keith Skinner showed these notes to Anne Graham who confirmed that she had tidied them up for Mike on the word processor

[top page faxed to Shirley H. - 5.1.1997]

from Shirley April 12th 1994.

Copy of 17 pages sent to Martin F - 13-5-1995

17 pages total

Copies to Shirley + Sally 23.1.97

Mike Barrett's research notes given to Shirley and Sally by Mike. July or August 1992. They have, however, been updated by Mike, on his word processor, with information and input from Shirley - (apparently not ... 14.4.99)

Transferring all my notes since August 1991.

ADDRESS

Address of Battlecrease House: 6 Riversdale Road,
Aigbuth,
Liverpool 17

(Morland, on page 14, refers to it as 6a Riversdale Road)

Address of Poste House: Cumberland street,
Liverpool 1

Michael Maybrick: Wellington Mansions,
Regent's Park,
London. Recorded in probate records 1889.

Edwin Maybrick: No address- lived in Liverpool- visited America - But do not know when and for how long.

Thomas Maybrick: 40 Dickinson Street,
Manchester. Recorded in probate records - 1889

William Maybrick : No address - lived in Liverpool

Alfred Brierley - Second lover of Florence Maybrick -: 60 Huskisson Street. - recorded in Liverpool Echo.

James Maybricks office: Knowsley Buildings - Off Tithebarn Street. - recorded in Liverpool Echo

Dr. Richard Humphreys: General Practitioner - No address.

Dr. Arther Hopper: No address.

Dr. Charles Fuller: No address.

George Smith - Possible address, Rhyl Street, will need to check if same George Smith.

Causeway Resources
(Historical Research)
8 The Causeway, Teddington
Middlesex, England
TW11 0HE

(1)

Revelent facts connected with Maybrick

Wife: Florence Elizabeth.

Maiden name: Chandler.

Born: Mobile, Alabama.

Mothers name: Caroline Elizabeth - Her third marriage was to a Baron von Roques - Nothing known about him.

Great-great granddaughter of the Reverend Benjamin Thurston - Nothing know about him.

She met James Maybrick on the ship 'Britannic' they were engaged within a week of meeting!!!

Married on 27 July 1881 at Saint James Church, Piccadilly, London - Not Saint James, Liverpool, as I first thought. (See Tales Of Liverpool)

One son: James Chandler, born on 24th March 1882.

One daughter: Gladys Evelyn, date of birth not known.

Facts on James Maybrick

Born: October 24th 1838 - Died on 11th of May 1889.

Father: William Maybrick - Born 15th April 1815. Died 28th of June 1870.

Mother: Susanna - Born September 1816. Died 1st May 1880.

Four brothers: William, Thomas, Edwin and Michael - Edwin is burried along with James and their mother and father at Anfield cemetry.

Causeway Resources
(Historical Research)
8 The Causeway, Teddington
Middlesex, England
TW11 0HE

(2)

Facts cont....

James Maybrick was a arsenic eater: Find out what affect arsenic has on the body.

He ends diary on the 3rd May 1889. The Liverpool Echo confirms he returns to his office - Knowsley Buildings - on this day.

Florence Maybrick had at least two lovers: One Alfred Brierly (a supposed friend of James) Fits in with diary ' A friend has turned'.

Find out about her first lover - Brierly, I'm sure was the second. To date nothing known.

Fact: Florence did have an affair with Brierly. Therefore if she had one lover, why not others?

FACTS ON BRIERLY

Florence first met him through James (Liverpool Echo).

She arranged two rooms (No 9 and No 16) at 'Flatmans Hotel, Cavendish Square, London'. On the 21st of March 1989, she arrived alone. Brierly joined her later. See Liverpool Echo - , the hotel porters statement, Alfred Schweisso.

He was a senior partner of Brierly and Wood, Cotton brokers - Liverpool Echo.

He was born in Lancashire. To date nothing more known.

Causeway Resources
(Historical Research)
8 The Causeway, Teddington
Middlesex, England
TW11 0HE

(3)

P.01

Causeway Resources
(Historical Research)
8 The Causeway, Teddington
Middlesex, England
TW11 0HE

QUESTIONS ON MAYBRICK

What was the name of his mistress? To date nothing known.

How many children did she have by him? - Five according to Liverpool Echo.

Did he change his will? - See last page of diary - 'I have readdressed the balance of my previous will'
Answer: Yes he did. See probate records 1889 - Library

Check for copy of 'Punch' around Sept, 1888 onwards - The first three letters of his surname - 'Turn round three times, and catch whom you MAY' - nothing to date.

Why did Michael and Thomas sell the furniture of Battlecrease before Florence was tried? Does not make sense when you read James Maybicks last will. They must have known something, but what? Did they sell Maybricks office furniture as well? (Nothing in Liverpool Echo).

Name of auctioneers: Messrs Branch and Leete, Hanover Gallery.

What items were sold? Nothing to date.

Where was Cotton Exchange? New Cotton Exchange off Tithebarn St. Built in approx 1917.

Where was Knowsley Buildings?
To date cannot find.

Reverting from Maybrick to the Ripper.

(4)

SEVEN RIPPER VICTIMS

Two victims unknown - killed in Manchester - one possibly early May 1888 or thereabouts. The second around December 1888 when Maybrick visited his brother Thomas.

KNOWN VICTIMS

Victim number two: Mary Anne Nichols

Known as Polly Nichols.

Born on 26 August 1845 in Shoe Lane, London.

Maiden name: Walker.

Married on the the 16th January 1864 to William Nichols, a printer's machinist. They live in a doss-house in Bouverie Street, London. They had five children.

The marriage ended in 1880 when Polly claimed that her husband had run of with the midwife following the birth of their fifth child.

Age on death 43. Buried on Thursday 6 September 1888 at Ilford cemetery.

Murdered in Bucks Row approximately around 3 30 am on Friday 31st August 1888. Body found by George Cross, a market porter on his way to work (1)- Police Constable 97J John Neil discovered the body several minutes later, but did not know George Cross had already gone for help - Neil sent for Dr. Ralph Llewellyn, who lived near Bucks Row - 152 Whitechaple Road (2)

The body was warm, a black bonnet lay near her. Inspector Helson of J division was detailed to attend the mortuary in Old Montague Street, in order to itemize Polly's possessions. He in turn alerted Scotland Yard and requested further assistance which arrived in the form of Inspector Spratling. Together both officees wrote a report which reads as follows:

Her throat had been cut from left to right, two distinct cuts being on the left side, the windpipe, gullet and spinal cord being cut through, a bruise apparently of a thumb being on the right lower jaw, also one on the left cheek. The abdomen had been cut open from centre of bottom of ribs, on the right side and under the pelvis to the left of the stomach, there the wound was jagged. The omentium, or coating of the stomach was also cut in several places and there was some small stabs on private parts, apparently done with a strong blade knife, supposed to have been done by some left-handed person, death almost nstantaneous. (3)

Causeway Resources
(Historical Research)
8 The Causeway, Teddington
Middlesex, England
TW11 OHE

(5)

THE DIARY

In it Maybrick says he was more than vexed when the head would not come off, also she opened like a ripe peach. He says he never took any organs away, but next time he would.

WHAT IS KNOWN ABOUT MARY ANNE NICHOLS

1. Maybrick had slashed through her jugular veins, windpipe and half her spinal column. In other words Maybrick had tried to cut her head off.

2. A large gash down the abdomen through which her intestines bulged. (Ripped like a ripe Peach).

3. No record of any part of her body having been taken away.

4. The report states that the throat and been cut from left to right. Supposed to have been done by some left-handed person. I do not believe Maybrick was left-handed - In the diary he says: 'I had to laugh, they have me down as left handed, a Doctor, a slaughterman and a Jew.'

---

(1) Page 36, Colin Wilson & Robin Odell: Jack the Ripper, summing up and verdict.

(2) Page 30, Jack the Ripper the Mystrery Solved by Paul Harrison.

(3) Page 32, as above.

Causeway Resources
(Historical Research)
8 The Causeway, Teddington
Middlesex, England
TW11 0HE

Victim number three: ANNIE CHAPMAN

Full name: Eliza Anne Chapman. (1)

Sometimes known as 'Dark Annie'.

For a time she lived with a man who made wire sieves, an association which earned her the nickname Siffey or Sievey (1).

Born in 1841. Brought up in and around London. Her father was a private in the 2nd Battalion of Lifeguards. (2)

Married on 1 May 1869 to a coachman named John Chapman. They had three children, one boy two girls. (2)

In 1882 John Chapman ended the marriage due to her promiscuous reputation. (3)

Age at death 47. Buried on Friday 14th September 1888 at Manor Park cemetry. (4)

Murdered in the back yard of number 29 Hanbury Street. Time of death not known, but it has been given as in the early hours of the morning of Saturday 8th September 1888. The body was found by John Davis, a market porter who lived with his wife and three sons in the third-floor front room of No 29. Davis reported his find, (along with two other men, who he had called to the scene) to Commercial Police Station. Inspector Joseph Chandler, the senior duty officer, took a verbal report, and then went immediately to Hanbury street. Telegrames were despatched to a number of police officers, including Detective Inspector Frederick Abberline. (5)

Dr. George Bagster Phillips, from 2 Spital Square, arrived on the scene and fomally pronounced Annie dead.

At the scene, according to Colin Wilson and Robin Odell, the following were found: A part of an envelope bearing the seal of the Sussex Regiment, on the reverse and on the front the letter 'M' and the post office frank mark 'London, 28 Aug 1888'. Also a piece of paper enclosing two pills. Close to Annies feet lay two rings, some pennies and two new farthings. * Note Maybrick does not mention the pennies. Why?*

Causeway Resources
(Historical Research)
8 The Causeway, Teddington
Middlesex, England
TW11 0HE

(7)

WHAT IS KNOWN ABOUT ANNIE CHAPMAN

1. Uterus was removed.

2. Maybrick tried like before to remove head.

3. Two rings were wrenched off her fingers.

4. Farthings, Two pills and the letter 'M' and two rings are mentioned by Colin Wilson and Robin Odell.

Question: Why doesn't Maybrick metion the pennies? Answer: I believe the pennies where a fabrication of the press at the time. See Paul Harrison book: Jack the Ripper, The Mystery Solved. On page 39, no mention of pennies. He being a policeman doing his research would not have missed such a fact. Therefore, if true, Maybrick would never mention pennies, which he does not.

Question: Why does Maybrick laugh in his rhyme? 'Along with M ha ha,'

Question: What was his clue? Answer: I believe he was the only one at the time who knew about the letter 'M'. Which is the reason why he laughs in the rhyme. I cannot find any reference to police reports, or newspaper reports mention it at the time. I believe the fact came out a great deal later. (I could be wrong).

(1) Page 44. Summing up and Verdict : Wilson - Odell.

(2) Page 39. Jack the Ripper : Paul Harrison.

(3) Page 40. As above.

(4) Page 47. As above.

(5) Page 42. Summing up and Verdict : Wilson - Odell.

Causeway Resources
(Historical Research)
8 The Causeway, Teddington
Middlesex, England
TW11 0HE

(8)

P.06

Causeway Resources
(Historical Research)
8 The Causeway, Teddington
Middlesex, England
TW11 0HE

Victim number four: ELIZABETH STRIDE

Full name: Elizabeth Stride

Known as Long Liz

Born in Torslanda, Sweden on the 27th November 1843 (1)

Maiden name: Gustaafsdotter

In 1865 she was registered by the Swedish authorities as a prostitute. In February 1866 she arrived in London and gained employment as a servant maid. In March 1869 she met John Thomas Stride whom she married. Stride was a carpenter by trade.

Murdered on or around 12.30 am the 30th September 1888. The body was found in Berner Street. At around 1.00 am Louis Diemschutz, a steward of the International working mens educational club in Berner Street, returned to the club with his pony and cart, as he turned into the court his pony shied and refused to walk on, after a second refusal he got down from the cart, sensing an obstruction in the darkness. In a split second of light provided by a match he saw a womans body (2). (see diary) Maybrick writes a rhyme "The horse went and shied".

In Elizabeth Stride's hand was a bag of cachous? - Dictionary description - CACHOU - an aromatic preparation in the form of a tablet or pellet, used to perfume the breath. Fits in with diary: "but I could still smell her sweet scented breath".

Dr. Frederick Blackwell - a local physician, arrived at 1.15 am and examined the woman whom he found to be dead from a deep cut in her throat. - Once again Maybrick tried to cut the head, he confirms this in the rhyme "I tried to cut off the head".

As far as Dr. Frederick Blackwell ascertains no other injuries were prominent. (2)

(1) Page 56, Jack the Ripper - Paul Harrison

(2) Page 53, Colin Wilson, Robin Odell

(2) Page 54, As above

(9)

CORONER'S INQUEST

Coroner: Mr Wynne E Baxter.

Part of the report:

'There were two distinct clean cuts on the body of the vertebrae on the left side of the spine, they were parallel to each other and separated by about half an inch. The muscular structure between the sides processes of the vertebrae had an appearance as if an attempt had been made to seprate the bones of the neck.' Once again Maybrick had tried to cut the head off.

Mr Baxter goes on to mention the missing uterus. * Note in the diary Maybrick does not mention what part of the body he took away with him.*

'The organ had been taken by one who knew where to find it'

This report implies Maybrick was a Doctor. Wrong!

THE DIARY

Maybrick writes his first rhyme: One dirty whore was looking for some gain.
Another dirty whore was looking for the same.

He says he was vexed when he had forgot his chalk and went back and cut some more. He says he took it away with him, and that it is in front of him and that he intends to fry it and eat it later. Three days later, after he says he has recovered he writes another rhyme, mentioning the farthings, a ring or two, the pills and the whores 'M'. He says: 'I will give them a clue.' He goes on to say he hated the whore wearing rings, and that it reminded him of his own whore (Meaning wife, Florence).

Causeway Resources
(Historical Research)
8 The Causeway, Teddington
Middlesex, England
TW11 0HE

(1c)

Victim number five: <u>CATHARINE EDDOWES</u>

Born : Gaisley Green, Wolverhampton on the 14th April 1842

Very little is known about Eddowes

On page 69/70 of Jack the Ripper the Mystery Solved it states - John Kelly a local labourer walked into the main foyer of Bishopsgate Police Station and informed the duty officer that he knew the identity of the Mitre Square victim (Eddowes). Kelly went on to tell the police that whilst reading a newspaper report of the crime, his attention had been drawn to the name of Emily Birrell. Kelly was taken to the mortuary where he viewed the body and positively identified it as being that of Catherine Eddowes / Catherine Conway.

John Kelly went on to say that he had met Eddowes seven years before her death in the lodgings of 55 Flower and Dean Street.

Other than that I havent found much more on Catherine Eddowes, however there is a great deal written about her injuries.

Murdered: On or around 1.44 am on the 30th September 1888.

Her body was found in Mitre Square by Police Constable 881 Edward Watkins. Police Constable James Harvey heard Constable Watkins whistle and arrived at the scene shortly afterwards.

He in turn was despatched to Bishopsgate Police Station. The duty inspector Edward Collard sent two constables to inform Dr. Sequira of Jewre Street and Gordon Brown, of Finsbury Circus, the official Divisional surgeons.

Dr. Sequira was the first official to arrive at the scene. The body was pronounced dead some 25 minutes later, this was due to Gordon Brown the Divisional Surgeon arriving late. After pronouncing life extinct the Doctors instructed the body to be removed to Golden Lane Mortuary. (1)

(1) Pages 60-61 Jack the Ripper - Paul Harrison

Extracts from surgeons report....(note in most of the Jack the Ripper books there is numerous pages on the report therefore I am just taking facts connected with the diary)

There was a deep cut over the bridge of her nose. Her face was very much mutilated. The right eyelid was cut through.

On each side of the cheek a cut had peeled up the skin, forming a triangular flap. (V) The left kidney had been removed.

Causeway Resources
(Historical Research)
8 The Causeway, Teddington
Middlesex, England
TW11 0HE

(11)

Eddowes, cont....

Maybrick says in the diary that 'they want a Jew then a Jew it shall be'.

He writes a rhyme :

The Juwes are
The men That
Will not
be Blamed
for nothing (Page 57 - Willson - Odell)

Question: Why does he spell JUWES this way?

Is this is funny little joke, which he refers to in the diary?

Causeway Resources
(Historical Research)
8 The Causeway, Teddington
Middlesex, England
TW11 0HE

(12)

THE DIARY

I am begining with certain parts of the rhyme:

"Sweet sugar and tea could have paid my small fee"

Fact: On page 67 Jack the Ripper/ Paul Harrison he quotes the inventory of Eddowes possessions: 1 tin box containing tea. I tin box containing sugar.

"By eating cold kidney for supper".

Fact: Left kidney taken.

Maybrick says he left Abberline a clue?

Implies Abberline has kept this fact away from the public. Quesion: What is this fact?

Quoting line from rhyme - "For I could not possibly redeem it here"

What is it that Abberline cannot redeem? On page 67 (inventory) it states - one Mustard tin containing two pawn tickets. Question: Was there more than 2 pawn tickets and Maybrick had taken one - hence redeem here? If so, how did Abberline know there was three pawn tickets?

Answer: Again on page 67 - "The pawn tickets which had been found in the mustard tin were traced to a Mr. Jones of Church Street, Spitalfields". Through the pawn tickets the police established the victims identity. Whose to say that when the police investigated the pawn tickets they discovered that Eddowes in fact had three pawn tickets and that one was missing from the tin and Abberline did not release this fact to the newspapers hoping that the Ripper would make the mistake of redeaming the ticket (although I have to admit this is unlikely). It would depend on what the pawned item was - was it valuable?

Note: That on page 67 Harrison says the police established the victims identity through the pawn tickets. But also note, that on page 69-70 of the same book, John Kelly came forward and identified the victim (is that a contradiction?)

Question: Once again if the diary is genuine then there is only one person who could have known about redeeming a pawn ticket (if I am correct) and that is Maybrick.

Maybrick says he has left a clue. In spite of what is written about the pawn ticket, I think the clue he left was his initial. Refer to the seconed last murder. Answers to why I have singled out the triangular flaps (V) refer to last murder.

(13)

Causeway Resources
(Historical Research)
8 The Causeway, Teddington
Middlesex, England
TW11 0HE

THE DIARY

In the diary Maybrick says that the thrill of being caught thrilled him more than cutting the whore.

Question: Who else other than the Ripper would have known that he was almost caught, also how would he know that the horse shied.

Answer: Not sure, but if the diary is genuine and written at that time these facts could have only been possibly known by the Ripper. Its a good point to remember that a great deal of the Ripper books were written after the 1950's.

Question: Could these facts have appeared in the newspapers at the time?

Answer: To date I have found no record of them doing so, however, a great deal of information must have appeared, but as yet cannot find anything, would have to go to London to find these facts.

WHAT IS KNOWN ABOUT ELIZABETH STRIDE

Coroner: Wynne Baxter commenced his summing up of the death of Elizabeth Stride on the 28th October 1888. He reminded the jury of the injuries to Stride's neck and how the windpipe had been severed causing the mass effusion of blood.

Elizabeth Stride was buried at East London Cemetry in grave number 15509.

Causeway Resources
(Historical Research)
8 The Causeway, Teddington
Middlesex, England
TW11 0HE

(14)

Victim number six: MARIE JEANETTE KELLY

Born: Limerick, Ireland

Date of Birth: Not Known.

Aged 25 - Married a Collier called Davies in 1879 he died in a pit explosion. Arrived in London 1884 (the youngest of Maybricks victims) (see diary "so young unlike I") (1)

Lived with one Joseph Barnett at No 13 Millers Court (scene of murder).

Murdered: Friday November 9th 1888 at 13 Millers Court, sometime early morning.

The body was discovered by Landlord John McCarthy's assistant, Thomas Bower, on an errand to collect rent. He discovered it when he peared through a filthy window. Bower ran back to McCarthy and they in turn informed Commercial Street Police station.

A telegramme was sent to Scotland Yard and Superintendent J. Arnold and Inspector Abberline were despatched accordingly (1) At 1.30 PM Arnold ordered the window removed, because the door was locked. John McCarthy was instructed to force open the door. The scene that greeted them was reported in the illustrated Police News and reads as follows:- (2)

"The throat had been cut across with a knife nearly severing the head from the body. The abdomen had been partly ripped open, and both of the breasts had been cut from the body, the left arm, like the head, hung to the body by the skin only. The nose had been cut off, the forehead skined, and the thighs down to the feet stripped of the flesh. The abodomen had been slashed with a knife across downwards, and the liver and entrails wrenched away. The entrails and other portions of the frame were missing, but the liver etc, it is said were found placed between the feet of the poor victim. The flesh from the thighs and legs, together with the breast and nose had been placed by the murderer on the table, and one of the hands of the dead woman had been pushed in her stomach."

Inquest October 4. (Shirley's hpmeting)

Causeway Resources
(Historical Research)
8 The Causeway, Teddington
Middlesex, England
TW11 0HE

(15)

THE DIARY

Note: - Maybrick states "regret I did not take any of it away with me"

See page. 90 Jack the Ripper the Mystery solved - Paul Harrison "It has generally been accepted that the Ripper took away all the missing organs, but this has never been proven, and it is more likely that he destroyed them by burning them on the fire, or cutting them in such tiny pieces that it was impossible for the authorities to identify them."

In all the books I have read no full medical report has proved that any part of the body was taken away, which in my mind suggests that Maybrick is telling the truth when he says "regret I did not take any of it away with me".

Questions regards the rhyme.

Maybrick says he had the key and he fled with it.

Fact: The door of number 13 Millers Court was locked and the key was missing.

Note: Abberline's enquiries led him to the conclusion that the key had been missing for some time, but there is no proof of this.

Maybrick says that he burnt a hat for light.

Fact: Clothes and the part remains of a hat were found in the remains of the fire, which fits in with "the hat I did burn for light I did yearn."(4) See page 88 - Wilson & Odell. ' Abberline believed the clothes and hat were burnt to see what he was doing. (Fits in)

"A handkerchief red led to the bed" See George Hutchinson statement on page 89 (Willson - Odell) Part of it reads:- 'He then pulled his handkerchief a red one out and gave it to her.'

Was it the handkerchief that he left in front for all eyes to see? Why has Maybrick underlined the word front? I have no answer to those two questions.

Why does he say "initial here initial there" ? Why did he underline ha ha after the initial M when he says in the rhyme "along with M ha ha" - M has to be is mark.

Causeway Resources
(Historical Research)
8 The Causeway, Teddington
Middlesex, England
TW11 0HE

(16)

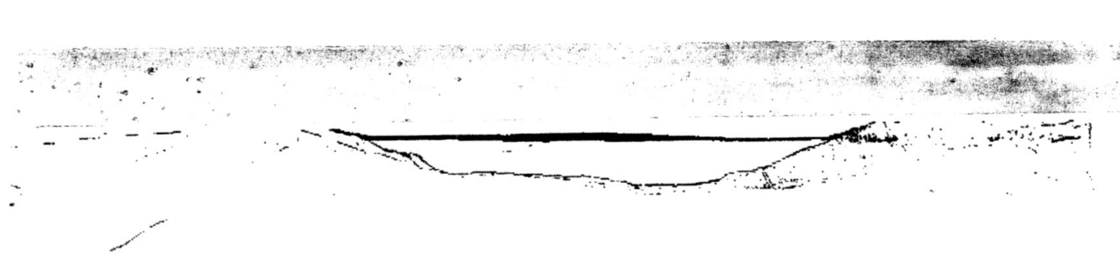

diary cont...

brick says he left his mark on Catharine Eddowes. The only
ks I can come up with are the triangular flaps about an inch
l a half on each cheek (V) Could he have been trying to carve
on her cheeks VV ?

otnote: Marie Jeanette Kelly was buried on the 18th November
88 at Leytonstone Cemetry, several thousand people attended
e funeral service. Page 91 Wilson and Odell.

1) Page 86 - Colin Wilson - Robin Odell

2) Page 79 - As above

(3) Page 77-78 As above

(4) Page 80 as above

Causeway Resources
(Historical Research)
8 The Causeway, Teddington
Middlesex, England
TW11 0HE

(17)

P.02

CHAPTER 6

'I'VE FOUND SOMETHING BENEATH THE FLOORBOARDS, I THINK IT COULD BE IMPORTANT.'

BY JAMES EDWARD JOHNSTON

Diary of Jack The Ripper "Original diary manuscript Copyright © Robert Smith, 1993"

'I've got Jack the Ripper's Diary, would you be interested in seeing it?'

Those were the words of 'Mr. Michael Williams', conveyed to an assistant at Rupert Crew Ltd., on Monday 9th March 1992. The assistant duly noted 'Mr. Williams' call and asked if he would ring back, when Mrs. Doreen Montgomery, then joint-managing director of the company was next available. Fortunately, 'Mr. Williams' did ring back, and it was from this unlikely scenario that the world would eventually come to know of 'The Diary of Jack the Ripper.' Now, twenty-five years since 'Mr. Williams' first acknowledged its existence, the Diary has come to the fore once again, inciting renewed debate as to its provenance, authorship and the mechanics of its creation. The purpose of this chapter is to present clearly the facts, testimonies and sequencing of events, which have been put forward to explain how the journal came into the possession of 'Mr. Williams'; otherwise known as Mr. Michael Barrett.

On Monday 13th April 1992, Michael Barrett travelled from his hometown, Liverpool, to London. At 11:30

a.m., he arrived, smartly dressed, at the central offices of Rupert Crew Ltd., ready to present the Diary in his possession to Doreen Montgomery. After initial introductions, he produced from a briefcase, held tightly beneath his arm, a document wrapped in brown paper, which was laid carefully on the office table. Montgomery, accompanied by friend and long-time client, Mrs. Shirley Harrison, remained silent. The document before them was a scrapbook, containing what Harrison later described as 'the most sensational words we had ever read.' As Montgomery and Harrison took turns to read through the document, Barrett talked them through the events and circumstances which had shaped his life – culminating in his acquisition of the journal now set before them. Then forty-years-old, Barrett grew up in Kirkdale, and had lived in Liverpool all his life. Having left school when he was fifteen, he had worked mostly in catering; on board ships and in restaurants, including a brief stint as a local barman. Most recently, until ill health had forced him to retire, he had been working in the scrap metal business. Now unemployed, Barrett was living at Number 12 Goldie Street, in the Anfield area of Liverpool, with his wife Anne and eleven-year-old daughter, Caroline.

But how was it, that the confessional 'diary' of the most infamous serial-killer in criminal history, came into the possession of an unemployed, ex-scrap metal dealer from Liverpool?

As recounted in Shirley Harrison's *The Diary of Jack the Ripper: The Chilling Confessions of James Maybrick,* Barrett declared that he had received the Diary from another Liverpool man, Tony Devereux. According to Barrett, in the months prior to his acquisition of the journal, he had developed an acquaintanceship with Devereux, a former compositor at the *Liverpool Echo*, whilst drinking at The Saddle Inn; a traditional public house located on the Fountains Road, Anfield. During the Christmas of 1990, Devereux fell outside his front door, fracturing his hip, and the resulting operation rendered him house-bound. In the months following, Devereux had entrusted Barrett to run small errands on his behalf. Then, in May 1991, during one of his many visits to Devereux's home, his friend, without preamble, presented Barrett with the journal. In an interview for a subsequent documentary about the Diary, conducted with writer/director Martin Howells, Barrett expanded upon his account;

> I struck up a three-year acquaintance with him [Devereux] and we became very, very good mates. I used to go down every day of the week, with his bread and his milk and his bottle of sherry, and I ended up going down there this one particular day, and he turned around to me and said; 'There you are Mick, there you are. That's for you.' I said; 'What the hell is it?', and he said; 'Take it home and do something with it', so I said; '...well what the hell is it?', and he said; 'Take it home and do something with it!'.

Barrett, according to his account, continued to question Devereux in the days following, pressurising him to reveal more about the document; 'How long had he had it? Where had it come from? All Tony would say was 'You are getting on my f**king nerves. I have given it to you because I know it is real and I know you will do something with it.' Eventually, Barrett said, Tony lost his temper when asked, 'Who else knows about it?' The reply: 'Absolutely no f**king bugger alive today.' Tony Devereux died at Walton Hospital on Thursday, 8th August 1991. With him, it was assumed, had died the key to the origins of the Diary. Recounting her initial impression of Barrett's account, Shirley Harrison wrote; 'On the face of it the Diary's pedigree was extremely doubtful. A former scrap-metal worker from Liverpool? A friend in a pub who was now dead?'

Barrett's 'Devereux provenance' was rejected outright by Tony Devereux's three daughters. Speaking to Martin Howells for the same documentary, Mrs. Nancy Steele (née Devereux) stated;

> The first we heard about this, Mike's original story was that my father handed him this parcel and said, 'I want you to take this for being so good to me and looking after me.' Well that was what Mike told me, but he [Devereux] had plenty of people, genuine people – family, looking after him. There is no way he would have given this to a relative stranger, who he'd only known for a couple of years on a casual basis, and sure his brother – if he ever did have this in his possession, and he didn't want to give it to us because of what it was, I'm sure he would have given to his brothers to sort out [...] Unless he [Barrett] can prove he got it off my father, I know we can't stop him, but unless he can say, 'here is the proof', then I don't think he should be using my dad's name.

The authors of *Ripper Diary: The Inside Story* also note that, before concluding the interview, Howells asked the daughters whether they thought that their father's name was being exploited by Barrett. Their response was intriguing; 'Oh definitely, definitely. He's making money out [of] a dead man's name as far as I'm concerned. I'm not saying that he's the only one involved because I think there's other people involved as well, but I don't know who they'd be. Possibly they knew me dad as well.' This raises the possibility that Devereux's daughters were, at least to some lesser extent, convinced that Barrett's 'Devereux provenance' was tendered as a means to prevent the Diary's true provenance, and thereby the identities of those implicated with its discovery, from ever coming to light.

So, if not from the hands of Tony Devereux, from whom might Michael Barrett have obtained the Diary? Where else might the document have originated, or have been discovered?

One place to consider is James Maybrick's former residence, Battlecrease House. Today known as Number 7 Riversdale Road, Battlecrease House is a large Victorian mansion, situated near to the banks of the River Mersey, in the suburb of Aigburth. When James Maybrick rented Battlecrease, it was divided into two parts. The Maybricks lived in number seven, whilst different tenants occupied number six. Latterly, each side of the house was further divided into two flats each, making four flats in total. Current owner of the house, Mr. Paul Dodd, acquired the property from his father; who purchased the premises for approximately £1,900 in 1946. According to Mr. Dodd;

> I don't even know precisely how my father came to buy it. I know it was damaged in the war because there was a [landmine or bomb] which knocked down most of the houses on the road, but this one was left standing, and I think the people who lived here before the war, for whatever reason, didn't return after the war – whether they had been killed, or, I don't really know, and so after the war I think the government had responsibility for buying property that was damaged and could do something with it, you know, do it up again, and my father availed himself of that and bought it at a cheap price. I think he paid £2,000 for it, or about.

Conceding that the 'electrics had always been a bit of a problem since moving in', Dodd decided to 'have a total rewire' and 'a new main [fitted] to the flat in 1989'. This included the installation of a new fuse board, an outdoor light fitted to the rear of the property, and a security alarm system. The contract, secured by Portus & Rhodes Fabrications Ltd., was carried out in two phases; the first rewire taking place in the ground-floor flat of the building, followed by a second rewire in the first-floor flat. The second phase of rewiring included the installation of night storage radiators; fitted over the course of three years, finishing in July 1992. Dodd recounted; 'Then, over a three-year period I had storage radiators fitted and a new ring main installed in the flat'. The electricians consigned to oversee this contract included; Arthur Rigby, James Coufopoulos, Edward Lyons, James Bowling, Graham Rhodes, Ronald Tennant, Roy McGregor, Brian Rawes and Alan Davies. It is important to note that these individuals were not assigned to Battlecrease House at the same time, but oversaw various aspects of the contract, at varying stages of completion, requisite upon their specific expertise and experience.

The initial phase of rewiring began in 1989, and took place in the ground-floor flat of the building and cellar. According to Dodd;

> There was very little need for them [Portus & Rhodes] to take any floorboards up [in the ground-floor flat] because basically what they did was very localised; tore abit of floorboard here and there I suppose, but at that time it wasn't really a 'floor job'; it was a kind of 'stick a drill down into the basement, drum the wire down from the socket into the basement and then take it along the basement ceiling'.

Furthermore, Dodd recalled that; 'he conducted much of the preparatory work himself', believing that the job 'required no more than three or four floorboards to be lifted'. As for the actual rewire, it is understood that much of the work was overseen by Arthur Rigby; who had been employed at Portus & Rhodes for a number of years. It was remembered by colleague Edward Lyons that; 'the firm used to send him [Rigby] out on all kinds of jobs on his own. He had been there the longest, and he was the 'odd jobs here, odd jobs there' kind of fella, you know.' Rigby was accompanied by colleagues Roy McGregor and Graham Rhodes – son of the firm's managing director, Colin Rhodes. Dodd later confirmed; 'Arthur Rigby, and the son…Colin Rhodes' son… Graham [Rhodes] yeah, him and…Roy McGregor, I remember those three doing a fair amount of the work on the ground-floor rewire.'

The second phase of rewiring took place in the Spring of 1992, and was conducted in the first-floor flat of the building. It was during this phase that the night storage radiators were installed, notably in the 'upper sitting-room'. This room had once served as James Maybrick's bedroom, next to his dressing room and study, and is believed to have been the room in which Maybrick died on Saturday, 11th May 1889. A requirement of the installation was to lift and remove the floorboards from the upper sitting-room. This was necessary to access the wires running beneath the floor and to install the storage radiators themselves. Dodd confirmed; 'they had to take the floorboards up because that's the way the wires were installed.' According to time-sheets obtained from Portus & Rhodes, Arthur Rigby and James Coufopoulos were tasked with removing the floorboards on the morning of Monday 9th March 1992. The time-sheets indicate that Arthur Rigby was at Battlecrease for approximately eight hours, while Coufopoulos was there only for two hours in the morning. It was during the removal of these floorboards that it is alleged, one of the men discovered the Diary. The journal is thought to have been concealed within a 'biscuit tin', which may also have contained a 'wedding ring' and possibly a 'gold pocket watch'. It has been averred that the journal was thrown into the firm's skip, located beneath the window of the room in which the men were working. In any case, it is thought that, upon reading the document and noticing the closing signature, the electricians opted to remove the journal from the premises of Riversdale Road, wrapping the document in brown paper or an old pillow case and concealing it beneath the front passenger seat of the vehicle which the men were using.

It is understood that, once removed from the premises of Riversdale Road, the journal quickly changed hands, eventually coming into the possession of Michael Barrett; known locally as 'Bongo'. It is thought that Barrett and Edward Lyons were known to one another through their mutual association with The Saddle Inn, which both men frequented. The pub itself stood less than five hundred yards from Lyons' front door, also on the Fountains Road, and less than fifteen minutes' walk away from Barrett's home at Number 12 Goldie Street. Lyons later recalled; 'I mean the house I lived in was only, I'd say five hundred yards away.' Walking from his home to The Saddle, Barrett would have passed Lyons' house on route. According to an article in *The Times* newspaper, published in April 1993; 'two [electricians from Portus & Rhodes] said they went drinking in The Saddle, where they might have talked about their work in the house famous for its murder [Battlecrease].'

It is probable that, as word circulated amongst The Saddle 'regulars' regarding the discovery, Barrett became involved with the journal on account of his previous 'forays' into the publication business. Truthfully, this did not amount to much more than a series of 'celebrity interviews' and word puzzles for D.C. Thomson children's magazine, *Look-in*, published in 1988. Given Barrett's reputation as a 'blagger', his claims of professional experience within the publication business were no doubt exaggerated. As reported in *The Telegraph* newspaper, publisher and current owner of the Diary, Robert Smith, surmises;

> Barrett was a colourful character who always boasted about being an author, so when the electricians at the house found this book, they believed he was the man who would be able to help them sell it to a publisher. The truth was that Barrett's only significant literary achievement was to write occasional puzzles for the weekly TV children's magazine, Look-in. Barrett had a highly impetuous nature. Just seeing or being told about the signature at the end of the diary would have been enough for him to reach for the phone.

Regardless of his true credentials, based upon the available circumstantial evidence, it appears likely that Barrett came to an informal agreement with one of the electricians, and thereafter assumed personal ownership of the journal. There is no indication that Barrett was made aware of the document's source, with respect to time and place of discovery.

Having acquired the Diary, on the very day it is thought to have been discovered, Barrett returned with the document to his home on Goldie Street. Convinced of the journal's historical value, Barrett decided to pursue publication; a decision that would, ultimately, have severe repercussions for his marital and family life. 'On that day, the Barretts' world was turned upside down. The Diary, which should have secured their happiness, was to destroy their marriage and prove the final straw for Michael's already fragile health.' That evening, using the pseudonym 'Mr. Williams', Barrett contacted Pan Books Ltd., hoping to sell the publication rights to the journal; his selection predicated on the fact that he 'owned several of their paperbacks'. Barrett's decision to use a false name was likely made on the presumption that he would not be taken seriously by the publisher, and that by adopting a pseudonym, he would be able to contact another publishing house without any record of a 'Mr. Barrett' having tried and failed to sell publication rights to the journal. It has also been suggested, that Barrett's use of an alias, in order to conceal his true identity, may have been attributable to suspicions that he was handling stolen property. Inevitably, Pan declined the offer and advised Barrett to enlist the services of a literary agent, recommending Doreen Montgomery – then joint managing director of Rupert Crew Ltd.; a respected literary agency based in London.

By January 1993, Mr. Paul Feldman, who had purchased the video rights to the journal in December 1992, had focused his attention on Battlecrease House. Feldman visited the property with members of his own research team, which then included crime historian Paul Begg and video producer Martin Howells. They were accompanied by Michael Barrett. In his book, *Jack the Ripper: The Final Chapter*, Feldman recounts;

> Paul Dodd had heard – from Shirley Harrison – that Maybrick's diary had recently been discovered. He went on to explain that new storage radiators had been installed in 1988 or 1989 [sic] Mike's reaction to Mr. Dodd's statement played on our minds for months. He visibly staggered backwards. Had something connected? (Feldman, 1997, pg.142).

There appears to have been some confusion, mainly on the part of Paul Feldman, as to which phase of the rewiring contract had purportedly resulted in the discovery of the journal. According to Paul Dodd; 'when Paul Feldman was investigating, he was convinced it was found in the ground floor, but the storage heaters were installed in the first floor.' As to which rewire necessitated the removal of floorboards; 'It was the upstairs rewire which is where the storage heaters were, that is definitely the case because there were no storage heaters fitted in that room in the ground floor. It was the first floor then, which would probably be around 1991/92.'

Aware of the direction in which Feldman's inquiries were progressing, Barrett made some effort, indepenantly of Feldman, to ascertain which electricians had been contracted at Battlecrease during the rewiring contract. On Wednesday 21st April 1993, Colin Rhodes, the managing director of Portus and Rhodes, received a phone call from a man claiming to own the Diary [Barrett] asking for information as to which electricians had been contracted at Battlecrease House. As this man would not divulge his own address or telephone number, Rhodes refused to give him any information relating to his employees. Barrett's inquiry suggests that he had not been made aware of the journal's exact time or place of discovery, upon his receipt of the document.

Shortly after these developments, Feldman records that he received a telephone call from one of the electricians thought to be implicated with the journal's discovery – Arthur Rigby. Feldman writes;

> One evening as I returned home from my office in Baker Street, together with Martin Howells, my wife informed me that a man with a Liverpool accent had telephoned wanting to speak with me [...] It was one of the electricians who had worked at Mr. Dodd's house. The chap shall remain nameless: I have no wish to embarrass him. He informed me that he overheard two of his colleagues, during a tea break while working at the house, mentioning 'something to do with Battlecrease.'"(Feldman, 1997, pg.143).

Continuing his account to Feldman, Rigby recalled how; 'he had been in the car with these colleagues and had noticed a parcel wrapped in brown paper under the front passenger seat. The journey took them to Liverpool University.' (Feldman, 1997, pg.143). It was surmised by Rigby that his colleagues were attempting to 'authenticate' the contents of the parcel. Rigby was 'asked to remain in the car.' According to Rigby's younger brother, one of the electricians claimed that the parcel contained a sample 'taken from his mother's pet dog' – which had recently died, and that he intended 'to get the sample tested'. Rigby's account, as relayed by his brother on an online discussion forum, is here reproduced in full;

> My brother [Arthur] never actually witnessed the finding of anything whilst he was working there. It was only the odd behaviour of the other two who went quiet in his presence and he saw them quickly put something that was in a pillow case or shopping bag under the seat in the van as he approached. The other electrician was giving him a lift into town but stopped at the university building at the top of Pembroke Place and took something in a bag. He told him his mother's dog had been ill and he was taking a sample of something to be examined. He remembers the names Alan Davies and Brian Rawes, they were not the other two who were working at the house.

It is clear from Arthur Rigby's aforementioned account, given to Paul Feldman, that he was convinced the Diary had indeed been removed from Battlecrease House; 'I remember something being thrown out of the window of the room where we were working at Mr. Dodd's house. It was put into the skip. With everything that I've since heard about the diary and considering the trip to Liverpool University, I think I've solved your problem.' (Feldman, 1997, pg.143). Feldman soon contacted Liverpool University, who confirmed that the two electricians had indeed visited the campus, but were unable or unwilling to provide any further detail; 'We contacted the Liverpool University. They recalled the visit of these two gentlemen. They could not confirm what they had seen was a diary, journal or anything similar. Unfortunately, they could not or would not tell me what they did examine.' (Feldman, 1997, pg.144). Arthur Rigby offered to verify his account on camera, provided that he remain unidentified; 'The electrician who had telephoned my home [Rigby] said he would go on video and state that it had been removed from Paul Dodd's house, provided he was not identified.' Regrettably, the proposition was never taken up. Speaking to the authors of *Ripper Diary: The Inside Story* in 2002, Feldman stated that, 'some electricians had taken documents found at Battlecrease House to Liverpool University', but that he had 'discovered they were letters unrelated to the journal.' This recollection is at variance with the reputed claim that 'the parcel' was animal related.

Following his conversation with Paul Dodd, and thereafter Arthur Rigby, Feldman contacted Edward Lyons and partner James Bowling, and accused them of removing the Diary from Battlecrease House. According to Feldman, Bowling denied having any involvement with the Diary, but disclosed that his colleague, Edward Lyons, frequently drank at The Saddle Inn. Feldman's account continues;

> I tried to telephone the electrician who lived near The Saddle [Lyons] – one of the two who had been identified by the man who had telephoned [Rigby]. I accused him of theft. He would neither admit or deny that he had removed the diary from the house. He continued, 'What is my confession worth?' (Feldman, 1997, pg.144-145).

When asked about this passage from Feldman's *The Final Chapter*, Lyons responded; 'Well that's up to him what he puts, but I fervently denied finding anything in that house [...] I think I did say to him it's quite possible it did come out the house [sic] Because it was that type of house. It was a really old house with book shelves all over the place, and half the house wasn't even being used.' In any case, Feldman interpreted Lyons' admission as confirmation that the journal had been removed from Battlecrease, and soon relayed this information back to Paul Dodd, seeking his permission to approach Barrett with a commercial deal. For a five-per-cent share of his projected royalties, Dodd would not contest Barrett's ownership of the Diary. Feldman recounts; 'Mike's reply was, 'Tell him to f**k off. The diary never came from the house.' Within twenty-four hours Mike Barrett had knocked on the door of said electrician [Lyons]; he accused him of lying and told him he would never do a deal.' (Feldman, 1997, pg.145). In a telephone conversation with this researcher, Lyons confirmed that Barrett had visited his home on the Fountains Road after receiving Feldman's proposal. As evidenced from this encounter, Barrett's chief concern was that should one of the electricians attest to having discovered or handled the Diary, his ownership of the document would be in jeopardy. Convinced that the journal was the 'real deal' and therefore of substantial monetary value, Barrett's urgency to smother Lyons' claims are not surprising. Feldman surmised that; 'The Diary had been stolen. Mike Barret was concerned that when this came out he would have to return the diary to Paul Dodd.' (Feldman, 1997, pg.144).

It was during this time that news of the Diary arose amongst the press, and it was widely reported that the document had indeed been found during the recent renovation work conducted at Battlecrease House. Covering the story for the *Daily Express*, journalist Philip Derbyshire reported;

Secrecy surrounds the latest bid to identify the Victorian mass murderer from what is claimed to be his diary – published later this year. But evidence points to James Maybrick who was poisoned by his wife Florence in 1889, a year after the Ripper's reign of terror in the East End. Maybrick was a wealthy merchant who made frequent business trips to London. His Diary was discovered two years ago under the floorboards of a house where it was thought to have lain untouched for 105 years.

Writing for the *Liverpool Daily Post*, journalists Harold Brough and Steve Brauner reported;

The diary is now owned by a former scrap metal dealer named Michael Barrett, but mystery surrounds how it came to light. One theory is that it was found in Maybrick's former home, Battlecrease House, Aigburth, during 1991 or 1992, although there is no suggestion that Barrett removed it.

At that time, major rewiring work was carried out on the three-story Victorian, semi-detached mansion on Riversdale Road, opposite Liverpool Cricket Club. The Daily Post has traced three of the electricians who worked on the house, all of whom deny finding the diary.

If it was removed from the house, Mr Dodd, deputy headmaster of a Liverpool primary school, believes he has the best claim to be its rightful owner. 'I'm not doing this for the money,' he said yesterday. 'I'm doing it because I would like to establish the truth. It must be certainly possible if not probable that the diary did come from the house. For my own satisfaction, I would like to establish which of the numerous rumours is true'.

The article continues;

Michael Barrett, the North Liverpool man who now has the diary, remained tight-lipped about Mr Dodd's claim yesterday. His solicitor, Richard Bark-Jones, of leading Liverpool firm Morecroft, Dawson & Garnett's, said; 'We have no comment to make on this.'

In an effort to repeal the intensifying speculation that the journal had been removed from Battlecrease, Barrett decided to swear an affidavit, on Monday 26th April 1993, in the presence of solicitor Richard Bark-Jones, that he had received the document from Tony Devereux. In summation, Barrett's disavowal of the journal's Battlecrease origin, and obstinate refusal to come to any such agreement with either Edward Lyons or Paul Dodd, was enough to persuade Feldman that the document must not have been removed by the electricians. Convinced that Barrett would have acknowledged the 'Battlecrease provenance' in exchange for five-per-cent of his projected royalties, Feldman concluded that Rigby and Lyons must have falsified their admissions in order to gain financially from him.

In October 1993, Scotland Yard launched a formal investigation, instigated by *The Sunday Times*, to ascertain whether Robert Smith, as managing-director of publishers Smith Gryphon Ltd., had attempted knowingly to sell a fraudulent document as genuine. According to Detective Sergeant Colin N. Thomas, who headed the investigation;

An allegation was made by the *Sunday Times* that a publisher who was offering the rights to the diary, had allegedly misrepresented certain facts, and the paper was alleging fraud, in that a contract drawn up did not allow them to interview certain people that may have caused them to withdraw and alter their opinion as to the genuineness of the document.'

News of the investigation was quickly trailed by the press. *The Daily Express* of Thursday 21st October reported;

Chapter 6

Scotland Yard yesterday launched an investigation into the controversial 'Jack the Ripper Diary'. Two detectives from the Organised Crime Squad will try to discover whether the diary is the biggest publishing hoax since the Hitler Diaries [...] The Diary is said to have been found under the floorboards of a Liverpool mansion.

One of the first individuals to be visited by the detectives was Michael Barrett. He was interviewed for approximately three hours on Friday 22nd October 1993, at his home on Goldie Street. In a series of emails to this researcher, DS Thomas detailed his own recollections of the interview;

When I interviewed Barrett in his front room, he was drinking cans of lager or something similar. His wife and father-in-law came in and went straight out of the room without speaking – they being a little surprised to see me and wanted to make themselves scarce.

Barrett as stated had a drink problem, and would not deviate from the fact that Devereux gave him the Diary in The Saddle pub, he was most insistent on this. As for signing his statement his words were; 'I will not sign it unless my QC is present'. When asked who his solicitors or QC were, he chose not to elaborate. This stuck in my mind as being a rather strange thing to say; people ask for a solicitor not a leading barrister. Perhaps he didn't know the difference or rather was trying to impress me, which he didn't. In any event, he refused to sign. At no time did he ask for a solicitor or any other person to be present during interview [...] he was interviewed as a witness not a suspect.

Barrett was not the only Liverpudlian to be interviewed by Scotland Yard. DS Thomas also visited Tony Devereux's three daughters; journalist Harold Brough; the landlord of The Saddle pub, where Devereux and Barrett first met; Paul Dodd, the owner of Battlecrease House; and several electricians who had worked on the house's rewiring. With respect to The Saddle landlord, Mr. Bob Lee, DS Thomas recalled;

The landlord who I spoke to, but who didn't want to give me a written statement (it would not have added anything to the enquiry) stated that Barrett was a perfect pest and a drunk and he was known to all, and called such as 'Bongo the Clown', and made a complete nuisance of himself with other customers, who treated him as the local idiot. It is possible that they [electricians from Portus & Rhodes] may have known him on the basis that he was in the pub when they were, but there was no indication that they had any conversation with him.'

Shirley Harrison received a similar account from Lee, when he was interviewed during one of her initial visits to Liverpool;

Tony [Devereux] used to come here regularly, long before he ever met Michael...Michael used to come in every day and sometimes he'd run errands for Tony when he was ill, but I don't think they got on particularly well. He didn't have friends. Tony's daughters used to come in too – nice ladies, they looked after their Dad. We never discussed the Diary in the pub afterwards...Tony was very quiet, he'd have never said a word. Tony'd never have given Michael anything he thought was valuable. I never saw the Diary – I didn't know anything about the Maybricks...I wasn't interested. You never ask questions in this job.

Barrett's dubious reputation among The Saddle 'regulars' was further borne out by Tony Devereux's three daughters, who were questioned by the detectives as to the likelihood of their father's involvement; 'I recall I spoke to the Devereux family [...] they were aware of that which Barrett had said, which was untrue, and stated the same views of him as the landlord of the pub. In fact, Barrett kept on ringing them about it.'

Cognisant of the reports alleging that the journal had been discovered and removed from Battlecrease House, the detectives also visited several of the electricians who had worked on the house's rewiring, including; Edward Lyons, James Bowling, Arthur Rigby, Brian Rawes and Alan Davies. Edward Lyons was interviewed by the detectives at his home on the Fountains Road. According to Lyons; 'Basically, in a roundabout way they were asking me where and what I had done in the house, and did I find anything. That was about it – they didn't mention any other guys or [...] Somebody mentioned Barrett to me.' With respect to Bowling and Rigby,

DS Thomas recounts;

> I recall speaking to them, and there was no mention at all about the University or any other matter. They were adamant nothing was found. It may be of interest that at some stage a young apprentice, whose name I can't recall was meant to have been working with them at Battlecrease. I made inquiries to speak with him but his mother rang me in my hotel room and gave me a load of abuse down the phone and told me her son had nothing to do with it and was not going to give any statement.'

The identity of the abovementioned 'apprentice' is uncertain. One candidate is James Coufopoulos. During a telephone conversation with this researcher, Coufopoulos confirmed that he was employed at Portus & Rhodes during 1992; recalling that 'he was quite young at the time'. He also confirmed that he had worked at Battlecrease doing 'a rewiring job' alongside Arthur Rigby. Timesheets obtained from Portus & Rhodes have confirmed that Coufopoulos was present with Rigby when floorboards were lifted on the morning of 9th March 1992.

Mr. Brian Rawes was interviewed by detectives on Thursday 21st October 1993. Rawes worked at Portus & Rhodes from December 1991, until he was made redundant on Tuesday 21st July 1992. Records of Rawes' interview and statement read;

> On 17th July 1992, went to Riversdale Road with man called Arthur to pick van up from premises. On arrival Arthur left, and Rawes went up to side entrance and called out, and Graham Rhodes and Eddie Lyons came out, took items out, and Graham, Colin's son, went back in house. Rawes got keys to van and Lyons said he had found a diary under the floorboards in the house, which he thought was important, and didn't know what to do. I got the impression he'd recently found it – I then drove back to the company.

Rawes' statement is an important feature of the alleged Battlecrease provenance. When interviewed by this researcher, Rawes expanded upon the details of his account;

> It was a Friday afternoon, and Colin Rhodes asked me and Arthur [Rigby] to go to this house [Battlecrease], and I didn't know where the house was. So, Arthur took me down to the house. Arthur shot back off to Colin Rhodes and I went into the house and told them that I needed the van [...] I was reversing out of the driveway of the house, and this Eddie Lyons told me he found this book under the floorboards and he didn't know what to do with it, and I said that I'm in a hurry so the best thing to do is to tell Colin Rhodes, because as I say, I never thought too much of it because I knew Colin Rhodes' son was there so I thought, probably, he knew about it as well.

The electricians which Rawes collected from the house included Edward Lyons and Graham Rhodes. This is supplemented by a timesheet collected from Portus & Rhodes, corresponding with the date in question – Friday 17th July 1992. Later that afternoon, Rawes was assigned to another contract at Halewood Police Station, working 'on the roof' alongside colleague Arthur Rigby. There, Rawes informed Rigby about his recent conversation with Lyons; recounting how Lyons had claimed to have discovered 'something important beneath the floorboards'. Rawes recalled; 'Well, we went to Halewood Police Station, to do some overhanging lights and while we were there, Arthur was on the ladder and I was on the roof, and I just turned around and said that Eddie Lyons had told me he'd found something in the house which was important.' Rawes believes that Lyons had in fact discovered and removed the journal some time prior to their conversation, stating; 'Eddie Lyons said he wasn't quite interested in it, and there was some other bloke looking after it.' Rawes was later able to develop this point;

> He [Lyons] must have found it before under the floorboards and whatever it was he had read and took it home and inspected it, and realised what it was [...] I heard that, the rumour was that it was at home [...] Eddie Lyons said he didn't want to really know about it and that someone else had decided to take it, or to own it, and it was the chap [Barrett] that went to the publishers in London.

Rawes' account was picked up by another electrician working for Portus & Rhodes, Mr. Alan Davies, who relayed the story to Mr. Alan Dodgson, owner of APS Security & Electrical Ltd., an electrical wholesaler located on the Northfield Road, Bootle. According to Mr. Dodgson's account, given in 1997;

> Alan Davies had come into the shop 'a few months' after the shop had opened in October 1991. He had told him how in a pub in Garston (near Mr. Davies' home), his 'partner' Eddie had said he had lifted some floorboards while doing rewiring work for Mr. Dodd, the deputy headmaster of a local school, who owns Battlecrease House. Eddie found under the floorboards a leather-bound diary, which was in a biscuit tin. Also with it was 'a gold ring'. 'A wedding ring.' Eddie, like Alan Davies, was employed by Portus & Rhodes, who had worked at Battlecrease House for Mr. Dodd on many occasions. However, Alan Davies was not working there at the time the diary was found.

Scotland Yard concluded the investigation and sent their report to the Crown Prosecution Service, claiming that the 'Diary was written post-1987 by an unknown hoaxer in Liverpool'. On Saturday 15th January 1994, the *Liverpool Daily Post* announced that the Crown Prosecution Service would be taking no further action against Robert Smith. The headline read; 'Yard Clears Diary Publisher of Fraud'. The Crown Prosecution Service informed Harold Brough that; 'We have decided against prosecution because there is not enough evidence to have a realistic prospect of getting a conviction.' A police spokesman from New Scotland Yard was quoted as saying; 'The Diary appears to have been cobbled together from three other books on the Ripper. The only mystery is who wrote the thing.'

As outlined in the opening paragraph, the purpose of this chapter is to present clearly the facts, testimonies and sequencing of events which have been put forward to explain how, 'The Diary of Jack the Ripper', likely came into the possession of Michael Barrett. Given the weight of circumstantial evidence, including the first-hand accounts of those directly involved, it is the opinion of this researcher that the journal was discovered and removed from Number 7 Riversdale Road, Aigburth, on Monday 9th March 1992, by one or more electricians working for Portus & Rhodes Fabrications Ltd. This opinion has been reached through an assimilation and assessment of existing research and documentation, as presented in; Shirley Harrison's *The Diary of Jack the Ripper: The Chilling Confessions of James Maybrick* (2010), Paul Feldman's *Jack the Ripper: The Final Chapter* (1997); Seth Linder, Caroline Morris & Keith Skinner's *Ripper Diary: The Inside Story* (2003); Bruce Robinson's *They All Love Jack: Busting the Ripper* (2015), and Robert Smith's *Twenty Five Years of The Diary of Jack the Ripper* (2017).

Bibliography & Sources

Chalmers, Robert, Jack the Ripper Revealed; They All Love Jack, Bruce Robinson, GQ Magazine, United Kingdom, Tuesday 6th October 2015
Feldman, Paul Howard, Jack the Ripper: The Final Chapter, Virgin Books, London, United Kingdom, 1997
Harrison, Shirley, The Diary of Jack the Ripper: The Chilling Confessions of James Maybrick, John Blake Publishing, London, United Kingdom, 2010
Evemy, Sally, Harrison, Shirley, Battlecrease, Portus & Rhodes Research Notes, London, United Kingdom, May 1997
Jones, Christopher, The Maybrick A-Z, Countyvise Ltd. Birkenhead, United Kingdom, 2008
Jones, Christopher, James Maybrick: The Most Controversial Jack the Ripper Suspect, Whitechapel Society 1888, London, United Kingdom, 2010
Linder, Seth, Morris, Caroline, Skinner, Keith, Ripper Diary: The Inside Story, Sutton Publishing, Phoenix Mill Thrupp, Gloucestershire, United Kingdom, 2003
Morris, Caroline, Response to Bill Beadle: Revisiting the Maybrick Diary, The Whitechapel Society Journal, Croydon, United Kingdom, October 2008
Robinson, Bruce, They All Love Jack: Busting the Ripper, 4th Estate, London, United Kingdom, October 2015
Smith, Robert, Twenty-Five Years of The Diary of Jack the Ripper, Mango Books, London, United Kingdom, September 2017
Smith, Robert, The Diary of Jack the Ripper: Twenty Years On, The Whitechapel Society Journal, Issue 52, United Kingdom, October 2013
Smith Robert, 'The Diary of Jack the Ripper; Report on Visit to Liverpool 29th/30th May 1997', London, United Kingdom, 1997
Whittington-Egan, Richard, Tales of Liverpool: Murder, Mayhem, Mystery, Gallery Press, Parkgate, South Wirral, United Kingdom, 1987
Newspaper Sources
Brough, Harold, 'Fresh Mystery in Jack the Ripper Diary Saga', Liverpool Daily Post, Liverpool, United Kingdom, 25th June 1993
Brough, Harold, Brauner, Steve, Liverpool Daily Post, Liverpool, United Kingdom, 24th June 1993
Brough, Harold, 'Yard Clears Diary Publisher of Fraud', Liverpool Daily Post, Liverpool, United Kingdom, 15th January 1994
Brough, Harold, 'How I Faked the Ripper Diary', Liverpool Daily Post, Liverpool, United Kingdom, 27th June 1994
Brough, Harold, 'Ripper Diary Forgery Claim 'Is Total Rubbish', Liverpool Daily Post, Liverpool, United Kingdom, 28th June 1994
Crowther, Steve, 'Ripper Diary Probe Launched by Yard', Daily Express, United Kingdom, 21st October 1993
Derbyshire, Philip, 'Diary Could Reveal Ripper', Daily Express, United Kingdom, 23rd April 1993
Evans, Martin, The Telegraph, 'Has the true identity of Jack the Ripper been revealed? Victorian Diary Proven Genuine Contains Huge Clue', London, United Kingdom, 6th August 2017
Fielding, James, Sunday Express, United Kingdom, 4th October 2015
Grey, Stephen, 'Mystery in True Ripper Tradition, Daily Express, United Kingdom, 5th October 1993
O'Flaherty, Michael, 'Ripper Book War', Daily Express, United Kingdom, 9th September 1993

Video Sources

Howells, Martin, Chris, Short, The Diary of Jack the Ripper; Beyond Reasonable Doubt? (1993, UK, Colour, 79 mins)
Robinson, Bruce, Shakespeare and Company Bookshop, 'Bruce Robinson on They All Love Jack: Busting the Ripper', (2016, France, Colour, 54 mins)

Interview Sources

Chapter 6

Coufopoulos, James, Monday 5th October 2015
Davies, Alan, Saturday 6th February 2016
Davies, Alan, Monday 15th February 2016
Davies, Alan, Sunday 2nd October 2016
Dodd, Paul, Tuesday 1st March 2016
Dodd, Paul, Thursday 6th October 2016
Dodgson, Alan, Tuesday 16th February 2016
Lyons, Edward, Thursday 29th September 2015
Lyons, Edward, Wednesday 17th February 2016
Lyons, Edward, Wednesday 24th February 2016
Rawes, Brian, Saturday 6th February 2016
Rawes, Brian, Friday 12th February 2016
Rawes, Brian, Friday 7th October 2016
Rhodes, Graham, Monday 1st August 2016

CHAPTER 7

THE MAYBRICK WATCH ARCHAEOLOGY IN GOLD

BY PAUL BUTLER

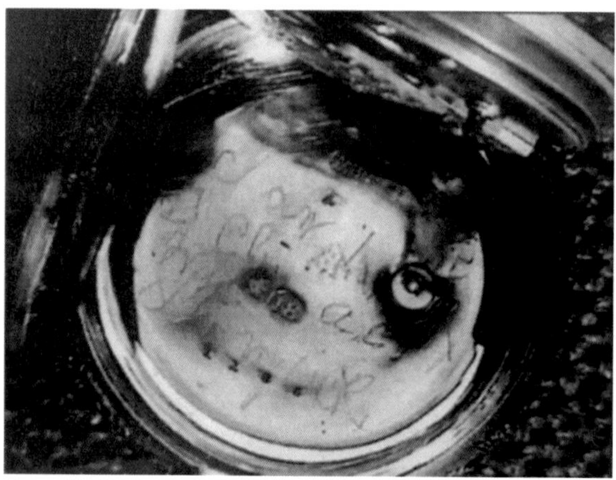

Inside the 'Jack The Ripper' Watch

The circumstances of the discovery of the 'Maybrick' watch with its tell-tale scratches comprising of 'J. Maybrick', 'I am Jack' and the initials of the five normally accepted Whitechapel victims is well known. Coming to light as it did, just as Shirley Harrison's book was going to press, got it off to a really bad start. The coincidence of its owner, the late Albert Johnson, discovering the scratches in the way he said he did understandably caused deep suspicions that this may be some sort of bandwagon hoax, cashing in on the interest caused by the discovery of the diary, which had then started to make the headlines.

To provide a little background, Albert's watch is an English, Lancashire made, mid 19th century, good but not exceptional, 18 carat gold cased, full plate fuse lever pocket watch. Quite a mouthful, it is probably a 'male' one and would NEVER have been worn by a lady as has been repeated with regular monotony over the years. Whoever picked this one out as raw material for his or her hoax, if that's what it is, made an excellent choice for a watch James Maybrick would likely have owned.

Victorian lady's watches, fob watches rather than pocket watches, are considerably smaller than Albert's watch at around only an inch or so in diameter, and worn either on a neck chain, a breast fob or chatelaine around the waist. Victorian ladies, other than a few very liberated ones, never wore a waistcoat and watch chain!

Having discovered the scratches deep inside the gold case, Albert paid for three separate sets of tests to be performed to see if anything could be discovered about when the scratches were made. The first two tests were made by Dr. Turgoose of UMIST on 10th August 1993 and 23rd August 1993, and the last by R. K. Wild of Bristol university on 31st January 1994.

Both Turgoose and Wild concluded from their separate testing that the 'Maybrick' scratches on the inside of the watch were likely to be at least several tens of years old, and that it would appear that they had not been made recently. Very encouraging for those that believe the watch has some history. But it is not the scientific findings that perhaps are of the greatest interest here, rather the discovery by the two experts of the order in which the scratches were made.

A little bit of explanation of what the markings are all about probably wouldn't go amiss here.

The part of the watch case where the marks are to be found is right inside in the most inaccessible place possible. It has been assumed by some, that the marks were found just inside the back cover, but this isn't so. In order to access them the front glass has to be released and hinged away from the face, then a small catch below the number six is depressed and the whole watch movement can be pulled out on a hinge. Only then can the innermost part of the case be revealed.

The scratches, which are all but invisible to the naked eye are tucked away where it would have been extremely difficult to make them, and where it would be the least likely for anyone in the future to discover them, if indeed their creator ever expected or wanted them to be discovered.

Aside from the various scratched markings, there are other stamped markings within the case, consisting of the usual set of hall marks and a stamped rather than engraved serial number. These will have been part of the manufacturing of the watch and will therefore date to the 1840s. We need not therefore be concerned with those.

Of much greater interest are the remaining markings which were scratched into the surface at different times and with various different implements. These have been described as engravings, but that term implies some sort of professionalism which for the so called Maybrick marks at least, is clearly not the case.

Anyone who has handled a fair number of antique watches will know that almost all contain various scratched numbers inside their cases, mostly meaningless to us today, but which were almost certainly put there by repairers in the past as a way of identifying their work at a later date. Some even claim the possibility that these were left by pawnbrokers.

Albert's watch has two such sets of comparatively neatly scratched marks, unrelated to the Maybrick marks. These are what appears to be H 9/3 and 1275.

Dr. Turgoose, using scanning electron microscopy was able to ascertain the order in which all of the scratches were made by seeing which scratches overlaid others and thereby building up a series of layers, much as an archaeologist does in the ground, so that he could date the various scratches absolutely in relation to one other, stating which were made first right up to the most recent. Wild agreed with Turgoose's findings.

Fascinatingly, the probable repair marks, H 9/3 and 1275, were both found to post-date the 'Maybrick' marks, which are in a lower layer. We know that Stewart's, the jewellers shop where Albert bought the watch, had it repaired not long before Albert bought it, so it had not been in working order for some time prior to that. Pocket watches, even those as grand as Albert's were worth more as scrap metal right up to the 1960s, and repairs are costly, so any previous repairs would very likely have been decades ago.

We know that the most recent repairer did not make either of the repair marks in the case, so this leaves us with the very real possibility that the watch has been cleaned or repaired at least three times since the 'Maybrick' scratches were put there. Any past repairs would most likely only have been done when the watch was still in use, up until most likely the 1920s when wrist watches became the norm, and old pocket watches ended up in the back of drawers or at the scrap metal dealers.

Furthermore, both experts agree that most of the random 'wear and tear' scratches also post-date the 'Maybrick' ones. It would seem then, that either the scratches were indeed made at least several decades ago, as the scientific tests would also indicate, or the hoaxer who put the scratches there was very sophisticated indeed, with in-depth knowledge sufficient to enable him to know of and engrave plausible repairer's marks, using a different implement and in a much neater hand, on top of his newly created 'Maybrick' scratches.

Whether the scratches were put there gradually over the decades, as seems most probable, with the Maybrick scratches amongst the very earliest, or in the space of an afternoon by an incredibly sophisticated hoaxer. The order in which the scratches were laid down is a matter of fact, and not one of scientific opinion, and for this reason should be considered very carefully when reaching an opinion about the likelihood of them being of a late nineteenth century origin.

CHAPTER 8

THE SCIENCE OF THE MAYBRICK WATCH:

THE TURGOOSE & SURFACE ANALYSIS REPORTS

PREPARED FOR A JOHNSON

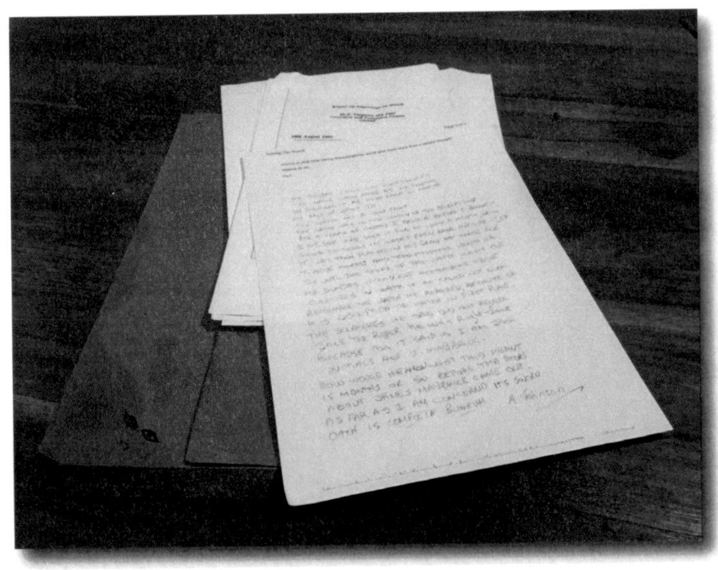

A.Johnsons Note Folder

Report on Engravings on Watch

Dr S. Turgoose MA PhD
Corrosion and Protection Centre
UMIST

10th August 1993

The views expressed in this document are those of the author alone. This document does not express the views of UMIST or of the Corrosion and Protection Centre.

Introduction

The aim of the study described below was to attempt to define the age of the engravings in the watch. From the outset it was not expected to be possible to provide definitive ages of the engravings, but an initial visual observation had indicated that it might be possible to discuss relative ages of the various markings and come to an opinion regarding the likely ages.

Experimental Studies

This report is of a scanning electron microscope examination of the inside of the back of the watch. This was to provide more detailed (higher magnification) visual observations with the possibility of elemental analysis at selected points. Photograph 1 attached shows a photograph of the inside of the watch, provided by Mr Johnson, and on the accompanying photocopy of this the regions of the other photographs are indicated.

Also indicated on this copy is the region (shaded) which it was not possible to examine due to the presence of the glass front still attached to the watch back. The presence of the glass has also compromised the resolution of some photographs and the quantification of analytical data, since the sample had to be further from the detector lenses than would have been desired. Nonetheless, significant information has been obtained.

Results

Micrograph 2 shows a low magnification view of the centre of the watch and the inscriptions. The horizontal marking, which is not apparent on the Photograph 1, is part of the large 'J'. This, and particularly the expanded view in Micrograph 3, show that the '9/3' was written after the horizontal line, and also that the superficial scratches are of later origin. An important observation arises here, will be seen in the other micrographs, and also is other regions

1

examined but not photographed. The markings identified to me as 'am J' and 'maybrick' are the earliest visible markings. All others overlay these where crossing does occur. Also all the superficial scratches are later than all the engraving. This can be clearly seen in Micrograph 3 where the random superficial scratches go across the engravings.

Another feature which will also be apparent in other regions is that there is very little evidence of 'mounding' of metal on either side of the horizontal marking, and that the scratch marks on the bottom of the engraving are very indistinct. The heavier markings such as the '/' shown vertically in Micrograph 3 show a degree of mounding but nonetheless a significant degree of smoothing of the surface of the mounds. The superficial scratches, however, appear to have sharp edges showing little smoothing.

From the central region Micrograph 4 shows that the 'S' is inscribed across the 'J', with other features as described above.

Micrograph 5 shows the central region of the 'copper plate H' showing similar features.

In the lower portion of the watch the 'y' is shown in Micrograph 6, with higher magnification in Micrograph 7. This shows that in places the engraving has been completely polished out, again indicating significant wear since the engraving.

Elsewhere one of the tick marks, Micrograph 8, again shows smoothing of the mounds and crossing superficial scratches.

Interesting features were seen in examination of the 'a', Micrograph 9, and 'k', Micrograph 10. Particles were seen in the bases of the scratches. These particles were of very similar appearance, although I regret that Micrograph 10 is not too clear on this, and the both gave only copper and zinc in X-ray analysis in the scanning electron microscope. It would seem that they are brass particles

2

and appear to have come from the inscribing tool. One feature of these is that they appear to have corroded surfaces, and again this may suggest some significant time since they were deposited.

Observations can also be made regarding the variety of implements used for the engravings. The 'am J' and 'maybrick' show no differences. The '1275' used a different tool and a different one again was used for the 'H 9/3'. The tick mark used yet another. The implement used for the 'ac' and 'mk' was different again but could have been the same for the two cases.

Since it was felt that fresh scratches might have a different surface composition from the older surface elemental analysis was carried out in and close to the base of the 'S', points A and B in Micrograph 11. Within the limits of resolution the compositions at both these points is similar, and consistent with 18 carat gold, so no conclusions can be drawn from these analyses

Conclusions

On the basis of the evidence above, especially the order in which the markings were made, it is clear that the engravings predate the vast majority of superficial surface scratches (all of those examined).

The wear apparent on many of the engravings, evidenced by the rounded edges of the markings and the 'polishing out' in places would indicate a substantial age for the engravings. The actual age would depend on the cleaning or polishing regime employed, and any definition of number of years has a great degree of uncertainty and to some extent must remain speculation. Given these qualifications I would be of the opinion that the engravings are likely to date back more than tens of years, and possibly much longer.

However, whilst there is no evidence which would indicate a recent (last few years) origin of the engravings, it must be stressed that there are no features

3

observed which conclusively prove the age of the engravings. They could have been produced recently and deliberately artificially aged by polishing, but this would have been a complex multistage process, using a variety of different tools, with intermediate polishing or artificial wearing stages. Also, many of the observed features are only resolved by the scanning electron microscope, not being readily apparent in optical microscopy, and so if they were of recent origin the engraver would had to be aware of the potential evidence available from this technique, indicating a considerable skill, and scientific awareness.

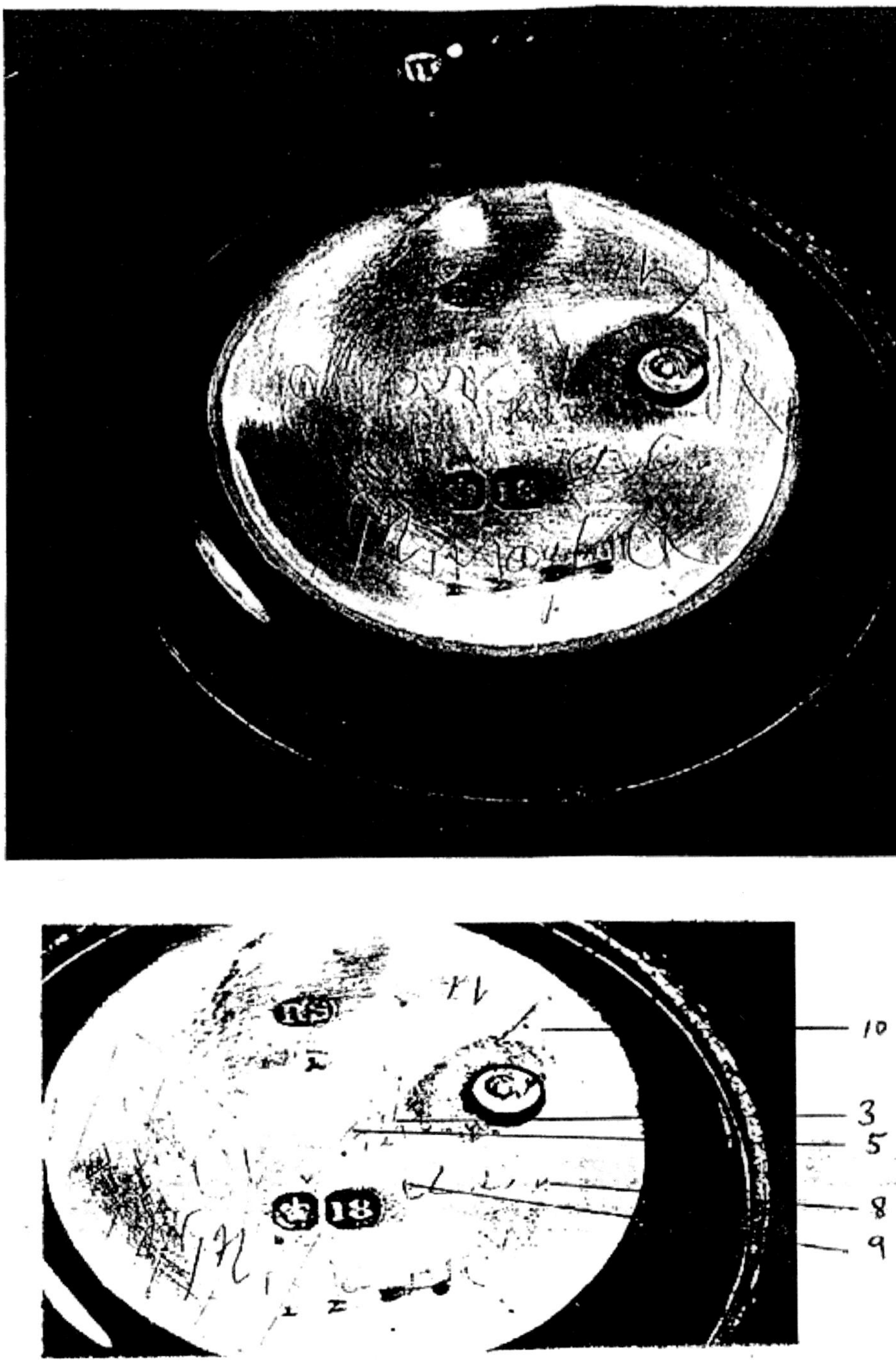

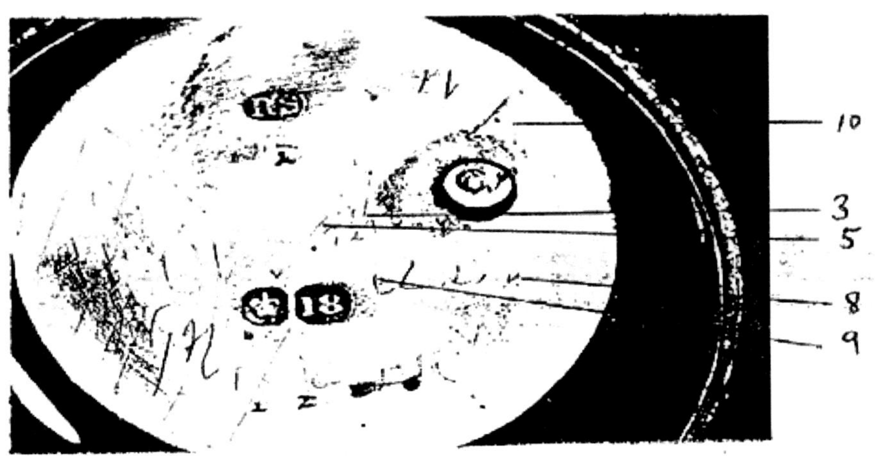

Photograph 1

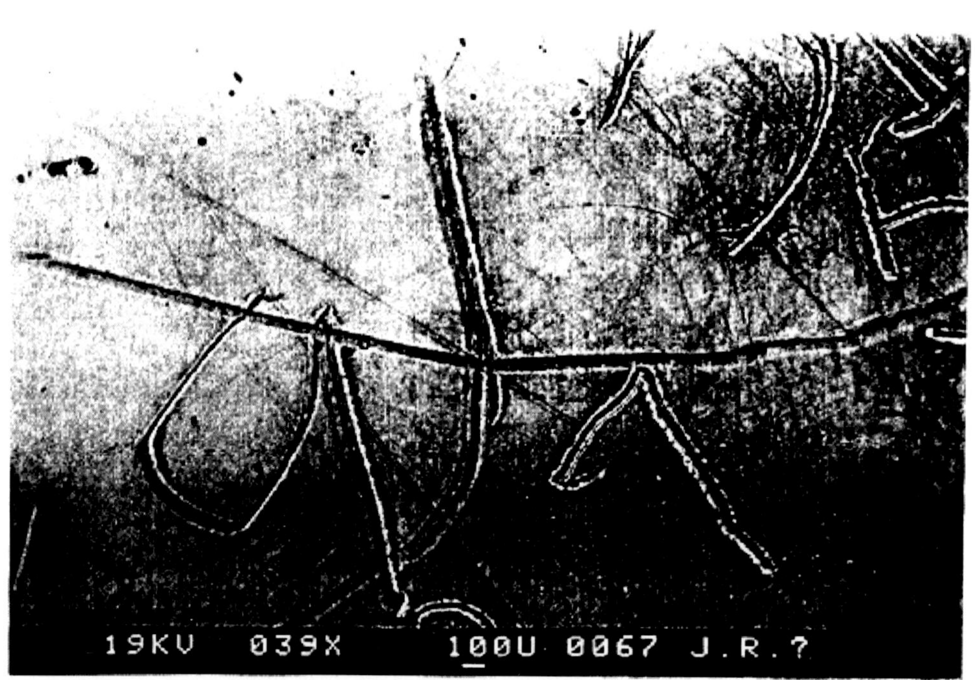

Micrograph 2

Micrograph 3

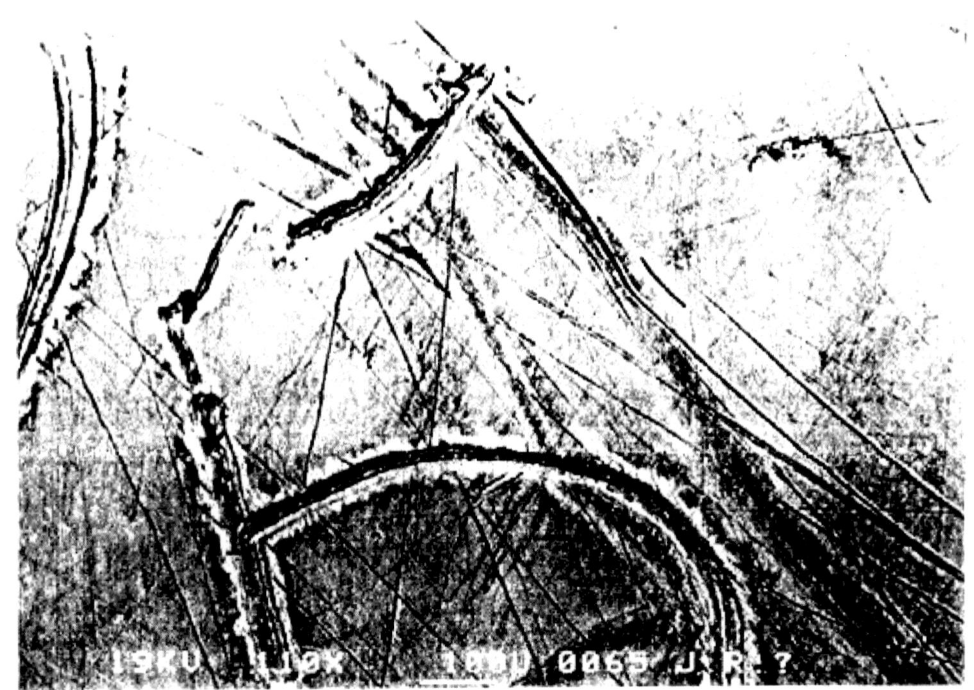

Micrograph 4

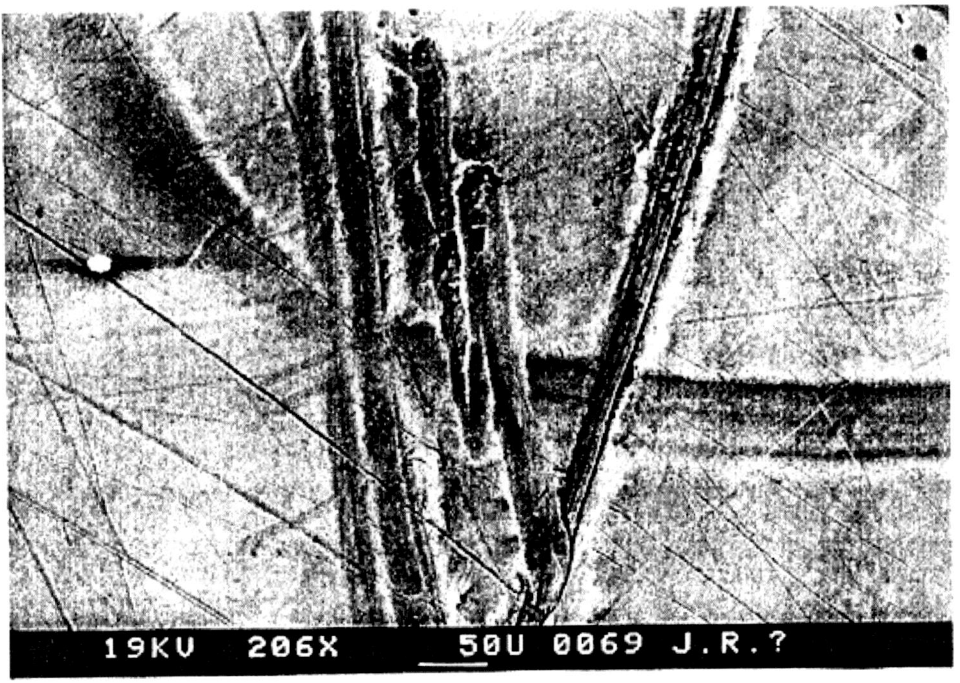

Micrograph 5

Micrograph 6

Micrograph 7

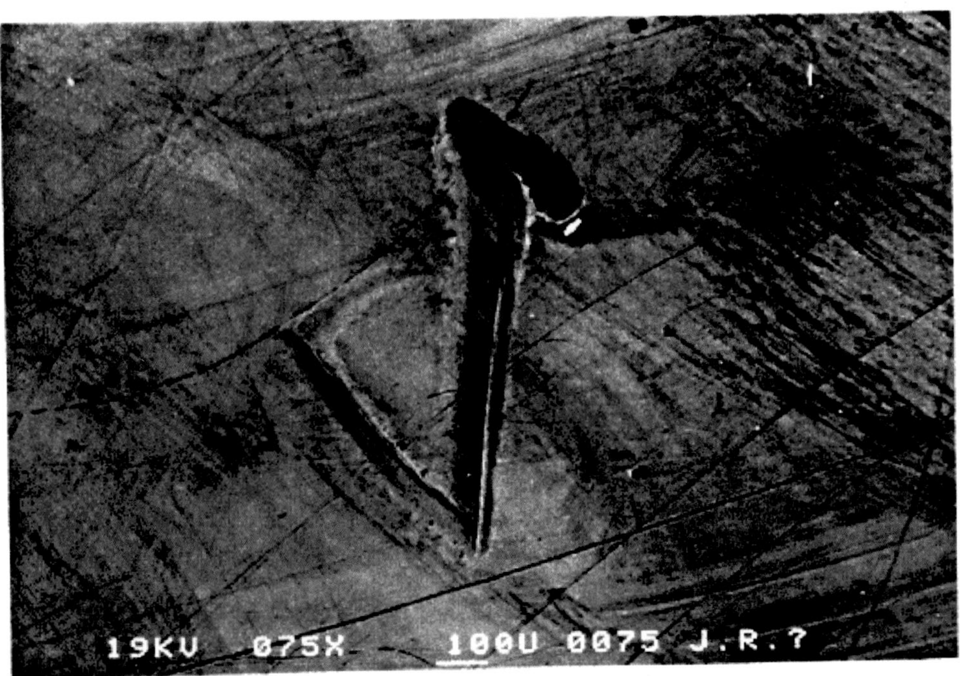

Micrograph 8

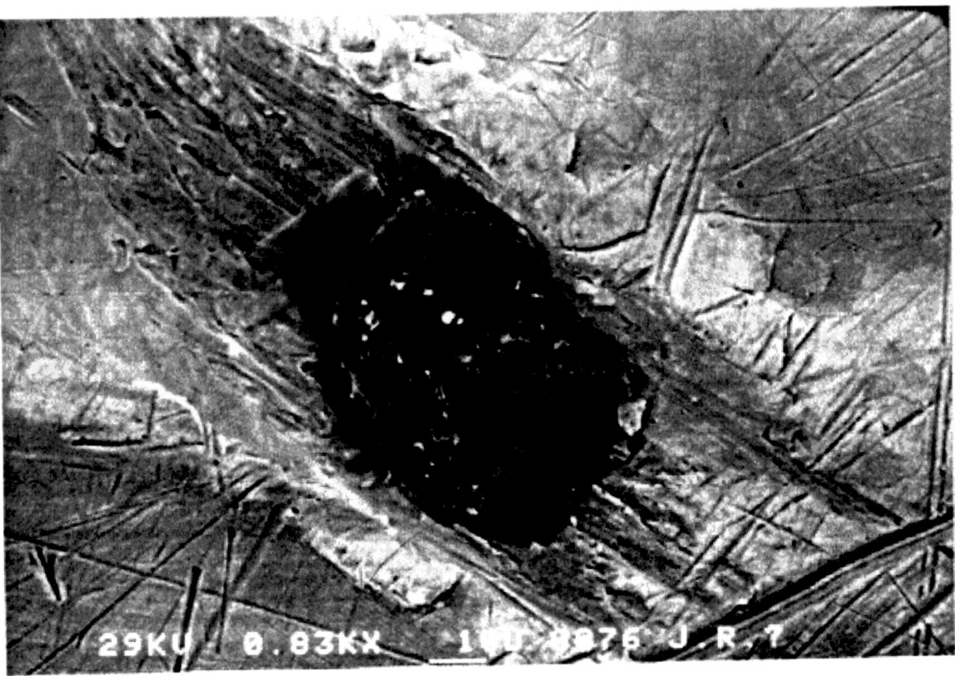

Micrograph 9

Micrograph 10

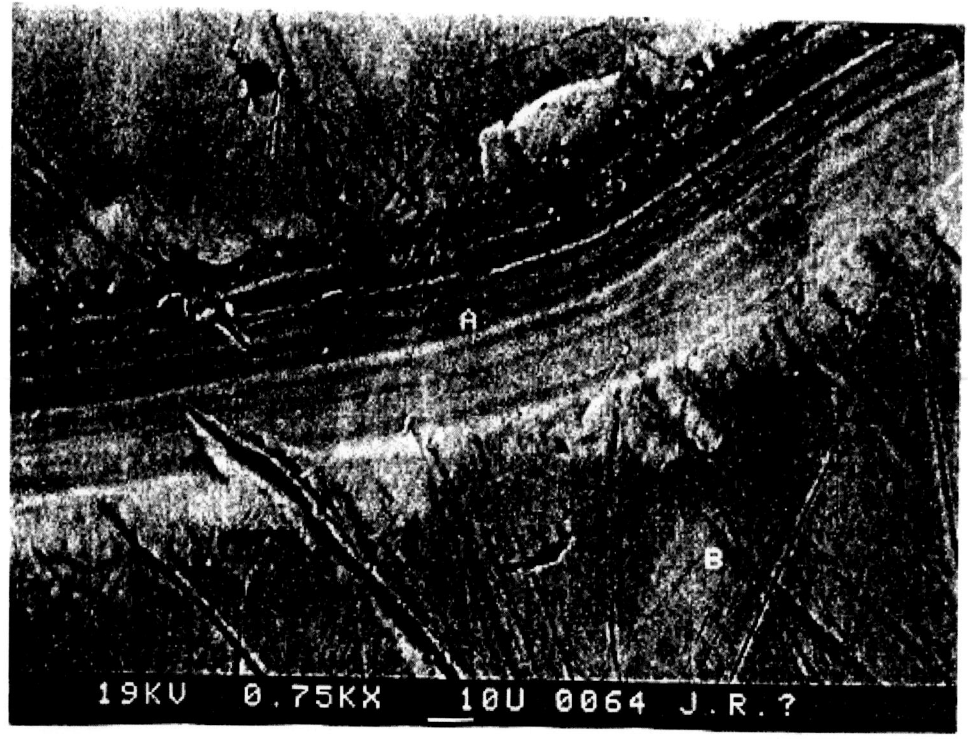

Micrograph 11

IAC/93/013
31 January 1994

Surface Analysis of a Gold Watch
Comparison of Original Surface & Scratch Marks

R K Wild

Interface Analysis Centre
Bristol University

Report prepared for Mr A Johnson

1. INTRODUCTION

This report describes some analysis carried out on a gold watch that was manufactured in the middle of the 19th century and which had some markings engraved on it. It was hoped that by analysing the surface of the original watch and the base of the scratch that an indication could be given of the date when the engraving had been made. The technique of scanning Auger microscopy (SAM) combined with argon ion depth profiling has been used to determine the surface composition as a function of depth. The amount of time the watch was available for examination was limited to only a few hours and as a result a thorough investigation was not possible and any conclusions are therefore preliminary at this stage.

2. SCANNING AUGER MICROSCOPY

The specimen surfaces are analysed using a technique known as Auger electron spectroscopy. In this technique the surface is bombarded with a focused beam of electrons with energy ranging from 2-10keV. This ionises atoms in the surface by ejection of an inner shell electron. The atom then rearranges with an electron, from an outer shell, falling into the initial hole. This releases energy which may be transferred to a third electron, which, if it has sufficient energy may be ejected from the surface. The energy of the Auger electron is given by:

$$E_{Auger} = E_1 - E_2 - E_3 - \phi$$

where E_1, E_2, E_3 are electron shell energies and ϕ is the surface work function.

This energy is unique to each atom and, thus, by determining the Auger electron energy the surface atom may be identified.

The Auger electron is energy analysed using either a cylindrical mirror analyser (CMA) or a hemispherical electrostatic analyser (HSA). The Perkin-Elmer PHI 595 has a CMA. A spectrum is obtained by counting the number of electrons in each channel within a predetermined range and can be displayed as raw data or massaged by computer. Most Auger electrons have energies from 0-2000eV which can only escape from the material if they originate in the top few atom layers. The technique is therefore highly surface sensitive.

3. EXPERIMENTAL

The engravings were on the back of the watch which was made from 18 carat gold. It had a diameter of approximately 4.5cm and was concave with the edges standing approximately 1cm proud of the base. The engravings were on the concave surface. This case was too large to be introduced to the spectrometer via the normal insertion port and since it could not be cut to size the spectrometer was vented to nitrogen, a side port with 200mm diameter was removed, and the case was attached to the specimen stage using copper wire. The port was then replaced and the system pumped down to a pressure of 1.10^{-7}torr. Ideally the pressure should be $<10^{-9}$torr but in the time available it was not possible to pump further. An area was then identified using the secondary electron image, which contained an engraving with a particle in the base and some original surface (Figures 1 and 2). Three points were identified on this area for detailed analysis. Point 1 was from the original surface, point 2 from the particle and point 3 from the base of the scratch. Auger spectra were then recorded from these points before and after surface etching.

RESULTS

The watch surface was heavily contaminated with hydrocarbons which were present as a result of prolonged exposure to the environment and handling. As a result the initial spectra only identified carbon and oxygen. The surface was therefore ion etched for 3 minutes which would remove approximately 100nm of the surface. Spectra were then recorded from three points; one on the watch surface (point 1), one on the brass particle (point 2) and one at the base of the engraving (point 3). Spectra from the watch surface (point 1), and the base of the engraving (point 3) are shown in Figures 3 and 4 respectively. These both contain peaks from gold at 60eV, carbon at 270eV, silver at 350eV, oxygen at 510eV and copper at 920eV. The initial etch did not clean the brass particle surface and only carbon and oxygen were detected. The spectrometer was then set to record the peak intensities from points 1-3 while the surface was ion etched for a further 20minutes, during which time approximately 600nm would be removed. Gold was not included in these profiles because the peak at 60eV sits on a steeply sloping background. These profiles are reproduced as Figure 5(a-c). It can be seen that profiles from points 1 and 3, the original surface and the base of the engraving, are similar. Carbon decreases rapidly with first silver and then copper increasing. The profile for point 2, the particle, shows no indication that the metal has been reached by the completion of the profile. Following the profile full spectra were recorded from these three points and these are reproduced as Figures 6(a-c). These show that there is still contamination on the surface as evidenced by the carbon peak at 270eV. However, spectra (a) and (c), points 1& 3 respectively, both show gold and silver peaks of similar peak height and the presence of some copper. The particle shows the appearance of peaks from zinc around 1000eV. The area was then etched for a further 20minutes, 43 minutes in total, and spectra recorded from these points once again. Again the spectra from points 1 and 3 were similar showing a further enhancement of gold at the expense of silver although some copper was still detected. The spectrum from point 2 still shows contamination although now the oxygen and zinc peaks have increased relative to the carbon. At this point this investigation was terminated.

DISCUSSION

It is the purpose of this investigation to attempt to estimate when the engraving was made on the surface of the gold watch. Two approaches are possible using surface analytical techniques. One involves analysing the two surfaces to determine if the composition varies with depth in the same or different ways on the engraved surface from the original surface. The other involves determining the amount of corrosion on the brass particles embedded in the engraved areas and attempting to estimate the length of time the particle would have to be exposed to give that level of corrosion.

The spectra from the gold surface and the engraved surface appear to indicate that the surface composition does indeed vary with depth. Silver appears to be enriched near to the surface with the concentration decreasing with depth. The rate of change of silver with depth appears to be similar on the original gold surface and the surface of the engraving, although the silver concentration at the base of the engraving appears to be slightly higher than on the watch surface . If this enrichment of silver occurs over a long period of time then this result would indicate that the engraving is of an age comparable with that of the watch. However, if this enrichment occurs in a short time scale and then stabilises nothing could be said about the age of the engraving. More work needs to be done to resolve this.

I understand that the watch surface was polished some six to ten years ago in an attempt to remove some of the scratches on the inside surface of the watch casing. This would have had the effect of removing some of the surface layers from the original surface but not from the base of the scratch. This could explain why the silver enrichment at the base of the engraving is greater than on the original watch surface and would indicate that the engraving was made before the watch surface was polished. This would indicate that the engraving was certainly older than ten years

The particles embedded in the base of the engraving are brass from the engraving tool (Ref. Turgoose, 1993). The particle investigated is very heavily contaminated and appears to have been considerably corroded. In this investigation the etching process, which was continued for some 45minutes, only began to reveal zinc oxide. This suggests that the particle has been embedded in the surface for some considerable time.

This discussion has assumed that the watch has remained at or close to room temperature throughout its life. The changes observed here would then indicate that the engravings were of some considerable age. Provided the watch has remained in a normal environment it would seem likely that the engravings were of several tens of years age. This would agree with the findings of Turgoose (1993) and in my opinion it is unlikely that anyone would have sufficient expertise to implant aged brass particles into the base of the engraving.

To give an accurate date to the watch from its surface composition and from the brass particles embedded in the base of the scratches it would be necessary to analyse several standards of known age, encompassing the age of the watch to recent time, of both brass and gold which had been known to have been exposed to similar conditions. This would involve a considerable amount of work.

CONCLUSION

From the limited amount of evidence that has been acquired it would appear that the engraving on the back of the watch has not been done recently and is at least several tens of years old but it is not possible to be more accurate without considerably more work.

REFERENCES

Turgoose S, 1993, Scanning electron microscopy examination of Engraving on Watch

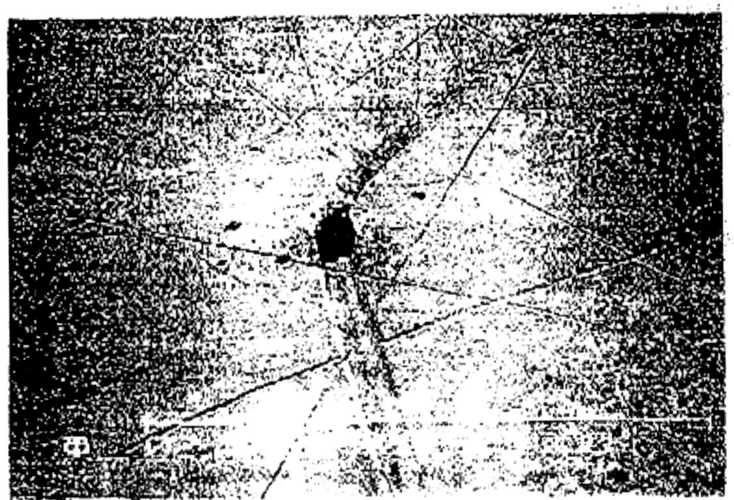

Figure 1. Secondary electron image of area of analysis on watch surface.

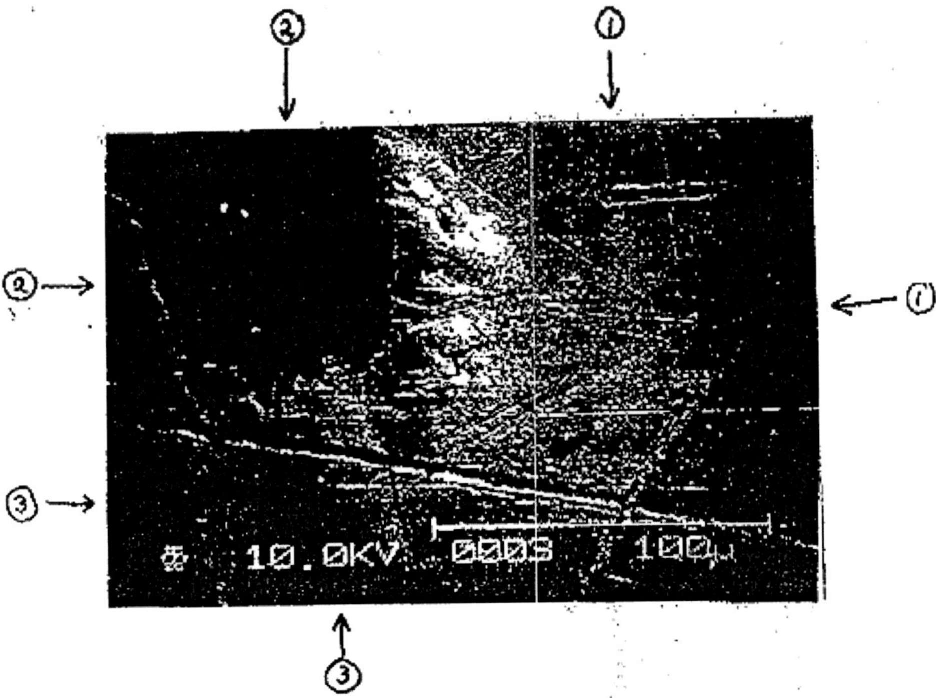

Figure 2. Secondary electron image of area of analysis with positions of points indicated.

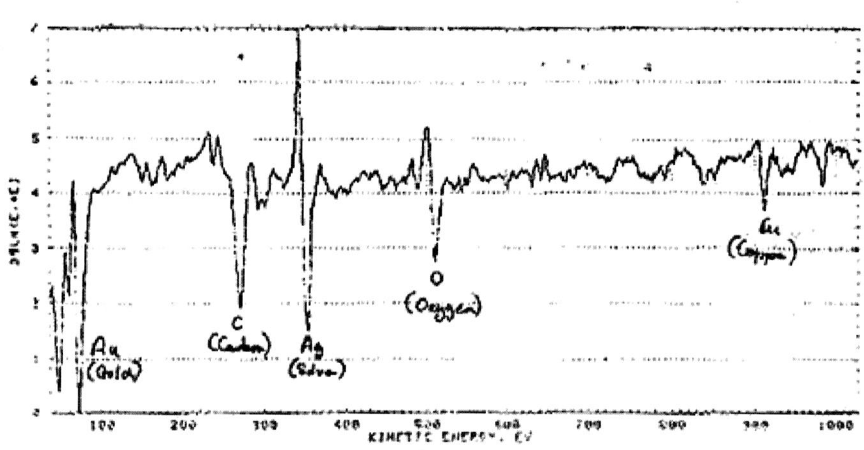

Figure 3. Auger spectrum from watch surface after 3minutes ion etching.

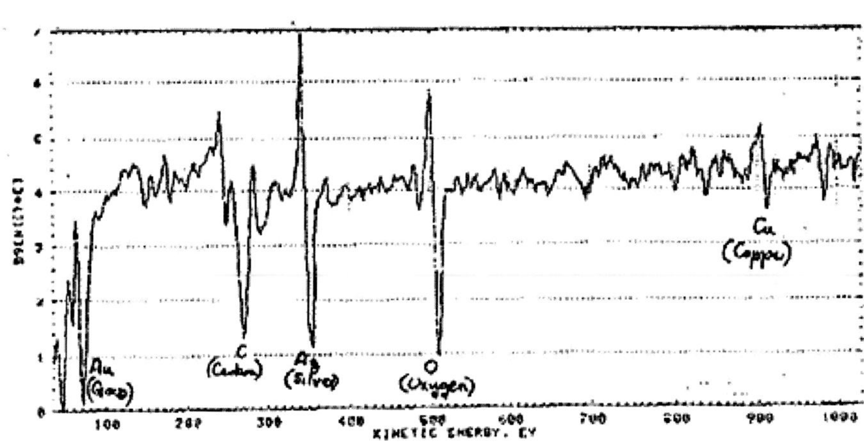

Figure 4. Auger spectrum from base of engraving following 3minutes etching.

7

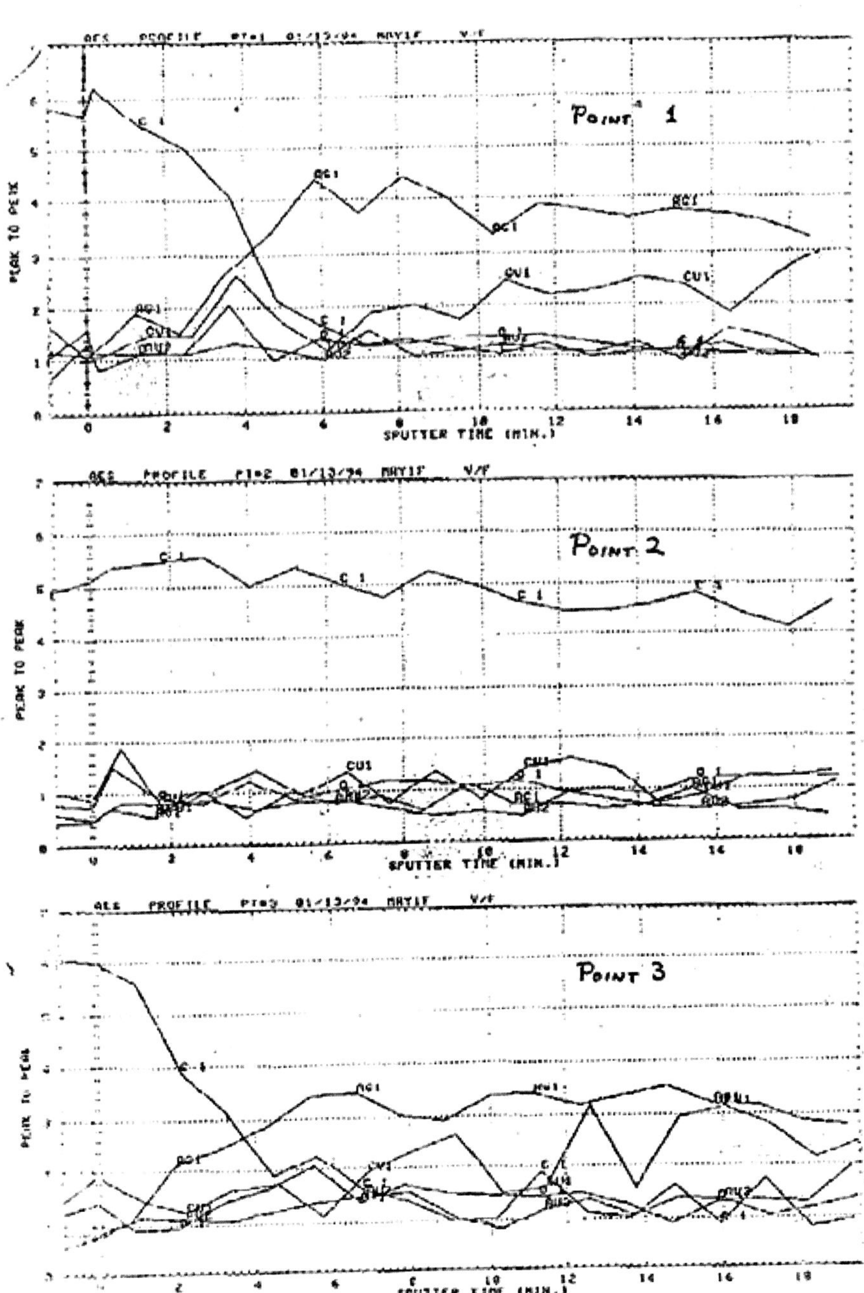

Figure 5. Depth profiles through surface of gold watch at points 1-3.

8

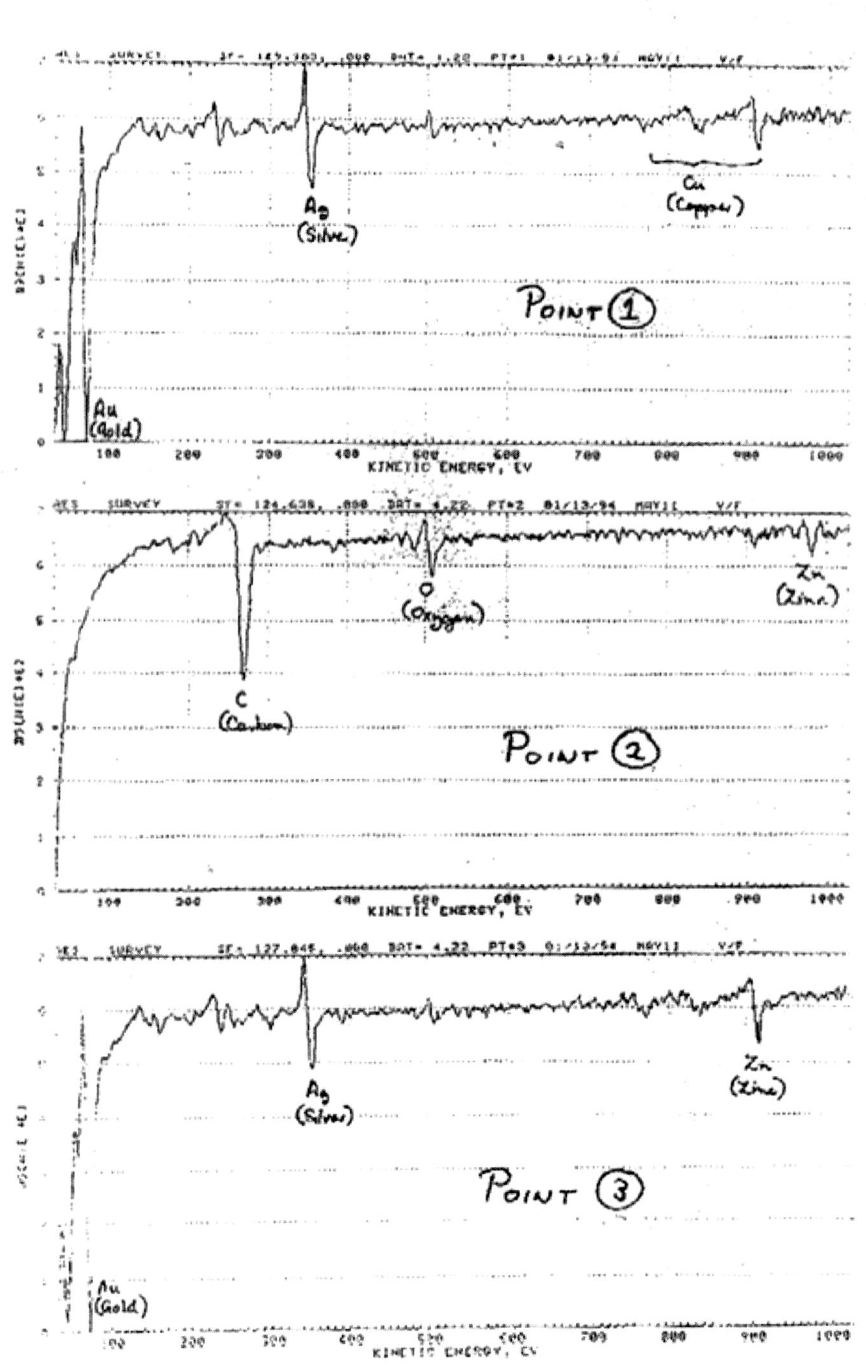

Figure 6. Spectra following 43minutes etching from points 1-3.

CHAPTER 9

NOTES MADE BY ALBERT JOHNSON, REGARDING THE GOLD WATCH

TRANSLATED BY RICHARD C COBB
DONATED BY DAISY O'QUIGLEY

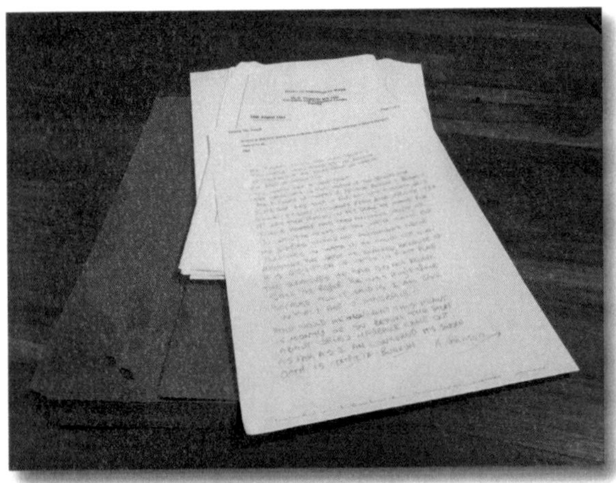

Albert Johnson's Notes

On 29th April 2017, I made a two-hour drive to Liverpool from my home in Cumbria, to meet with a young woman named Daisy O'Quigley, the Granddaughter of the late Albert Johnson. She was up until then, only known to me by a few brief exchanges on social media, where we had discussed the upcoming 2017 conference in Liverpool and of course the elephant in the room when it comes to the Maybrick Diary story, the gold watch.

As explained earlier in this book, it was her Grandfather, Albert, who had bought the now famous, watch from a Liverpool Jewellers, for the price of £225, on Tuesday 14th July 1992, and it was he who first noticed unusual scratch marks inside the back cover, and under closer inspection the words; I AM JACK, initials of the canonical five victims and J. Maybrick. We met up in a pub near to where daisy lives, and after some discussion she presented me with a red paper folder, formerly owned by her grandfather that contained a range of papers. She had found this paper folder stored in a drawer and thought it might be of some importance and wanted to share it with me. The papers were mostly print outs of arguments, conversations and debates from a 2005 thread on the Jack the Ripper forum website, Casebook, entitled "Testing the Watch".

As expected the print outs contained conversations between forum members debating the issue of provenance, sworn statements and the tests that had been carried out. Some called into question Albert's honesty and not surprisingly one of the main points was how could anyone even see those tiny scratches in the watch unless you knew to look for them. Well it seems, Albert printed out these sheets and added his own handwritten notes to answer some of the questions. These notes I am assuming, were never meant to see the light of day and it is only thanks to Daisy that we can see some of his responses.

Note: 1

Testing The W[illegible] Page 1 of 1

Testing The Watch

Casebook: Jack the Ripper - Message Boards: Suspects: Maybrick, James: The "Maybrick" Watch: Testing The Watch

Posted by on **Friday, February 25, 2005 - 9:37 am**:

"I have seen it once, in Bournemouth, knowing the ripper marks were there, but still not being able to see them with an ordinary magnifying glass;"

This, to me, is one of the more intriguing angles of the case; personally, I think a hoaxer would have made the scratches a tad more visible. Actually, let me more specific: I think a hoaxer intending for their hoax to be "discovered" would have made bolder scratches.

Of course, th[illegible] [illegible]ises another question: if you couldn't see them, despite knowing they were there, how [illegible] [illegible]rt and his buddies see them?

The clot[illegible] [illegible]kens...

BRIGHT LIGHT COMING THROUGH WINDOW
WHILE HAVING BREAK. IT WAS coincidence
THE LETTERS WERE SEEN, AND CURIOSITY
WAS TO LOOK AT THROUGH MICROSCOPE AT COLLEGE.
A BEGINNING TO A VERY VERY LONG STORY.

http://casebook.org/cgi-bin/forum/board-admin.cgi?action=quick&do=print&HTTP_... 04/03/2005

In response to one forum member who says –

"I have seen it (Watch) once, in Bournemouth, knowing the ripper marks were there, but still not being able to see them with an ordinary magnifying glass; this to me, is one of the more intriguing angles of the case; personally, I think a hoaxer intending for their hoax to be discovered would have made bolder scratches. Of course, this raises another question: if you couldn't see them, despite knowing they were there, how did Albert and his buddies see them?

Albert writes below in pencil -

"While having break. It was coincidence
The letters were seen, and curiosity
Was to look at through microscope at college
A beginning to a very very long story."

Note: 2

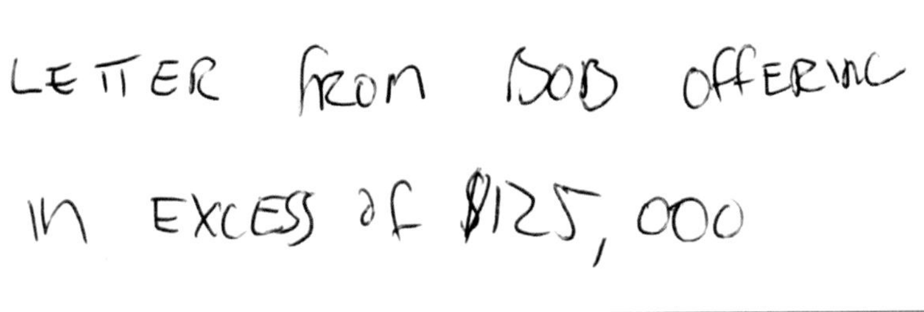

Another issue raised by those who are critical of Albert Johnson, is that he was hoping to make some money from jumping on the back of the diary story. So, he faked the watch to cash in on the media frenzy? However, we don't see this happening.

On 28th July 1993 Albert and his brother Robbie take the watch to Dr. Stephen Turgoose of the Corrosion Protection Centre, at University of Manchester Institute of Science and Technology. They have the watch tested at their own expense of several hundred pounds. Not exactly the actions of a would-be forger. They also volunteered the watch for a second independent test in January 1994, both times the results were in favour of the watch being genuine.

Albert – who was living on a very modest wage was also known to have turned down an offer of $40,000 for the watch. Some have suggested he was a gambling man who wanted to hold out for a better offer, yet according to a handwritten note in his papers he also "appears" to have turned down an incredible offer of $125,000, from someone called Bob.

Albert writes in black pen –

"LETTER FROM BOB OFFERING IN EXCESS OF $125,000"

It seems, he simply wasn't as interested in money, as he was for the truth.

Note: 3

During the early days of the watch's discovery, Stanley Dangar, a watch expert from North East Spain came to England to conduct an examination of his own. He was far more critical of the Watch and went so far as to attempt a scientific test to show how it was possible to fake the age of the scratches and make it appear older than it actually was. These tests failed to deliver his desired results. Not to be outdone he then hired a private detective to take a statement from a Mr. Tim Dundas, a watch repairer from 'The Clock Workshop', West Kirby, Wirral. Mr. Dundas had worked on many watches for local jewellers before they were then returned back to the shops to be sold. Mr. Tim Dundas had also allegedly repaired the watch in question, just prior to Albert Johnson purchasing it.

The statement from Mr. Dundas, which then appeared on the internet, said that when he cleaned the watch there were no scratches.

"The marks on the watch relating to "Jack the Ripper" have been made on the watch since I examined and repaired it in 1992, the whole suggestion that this watch belonged to "Jack the Ripper" is completely false."

However, it seems Mr. Dundas may have been mistaken with which watch he was referring to. After all several watches had been sent to him for repair, and as far as he was concerned the watch he remembered, had a white/silver face with the words "Verity" on the front. This is not an accurate description of Albert's watch. One must also take into consideration the statement of Mr. Ron Murphy from Stewarts the jewelers, who claimed he had seen the scratches himself and tried polishing them out before putting it in the shop window for sale. Albert himself seems to have replied in a hand-written note made in pencil and found among his papers, this note he even signs his name.

He says –

"Mr. Dundas could not even identify the watch when asked by Mr. Feldman, he described it as silver front no marking on back of watch to. The watch has a gold front The watch was in the window of the jeweler's shop for a couple of months I believe before I bought it, I myself had seen it for at least a month, while going to collect my wages from bank opposite. TSB It was then placed in my drawer at home for twelve months and then another month or so until the story of the watch came out. Mr. Dundas would not remember about scratches in watch if he could not even remember the watch he repaired, because of this description of watch in first place. The scratches he said did not reveal Jack the Ripper, he was right there because all it said is I am Jack, initials and J.Maybrick. How would he know what this meant 15 months or so before the story about James Maybrick came out. As far as I am concerned his sworn oath is complete Bunkum.
A. Johnson"

Conclusion

I hope these notes are useful for anyone wanting to understand a little bit more of the mind of Albert Johnson. Why these notes were made, I do not know, perhaps research will uncover more notes and correspondents which can shed further light on the matter. For now, I'm willing to say the watch is a very much, an over looked piece of a puzzle which should by all rights, be taken more seriously. It has stood up to all the scientific tests, and at time of writing has yet to be proved anything other than genuine.

The feeling that it all sounds too good to be true, isn't really sufficient evidence to declare that the watch is a modern forgery. I find highly unlikely that anyone who knew the watch was not the genuine article, would write down these pencil notes in a private response. Or that they would spend hundreds of pounds of their own money, having it independently tested to prove authenticity, to then turn down huge cash offers to buy the watch in-between.

So, until new evidence comes to light, it would seem, for now anyway, the watch is still ticking loudly away, amongst the silence of its critics.

Watch owner the late Albert Johnson

anyone at that time seeing those scratches would give them more than a second thought?

regards to all,

Paul

MR. DUNDAS, COULD NOT EVEN EDENTIFY
THE WATCH WHEN ASKED BY MR FELDMAN,
HE DISCRIBED IT AS SILVER FRONT NO MARKING
ON BACK OF WATCH J.O.
THE WATCH HAS A GOLD FRONT.
THE WATCH WAS IN THE WINDOW OF THE JEWLERS SHOP
FOR A COUPLE OF MONTHS I BELIEVE BEFORE I BOUGHT IT,
I MY SELF HAD SEEN IT FOR AT LEAST A MONTH, WHILE
GOING TO COLLECT MY WAGES FROM BANK OPPISITE - TSB
IT WAS THEN PLACED IN MY DRAW AT HOME FOR
TWELVE MONTHS AND THEN ANOTHER MONTH OR
SO UNTIL THE STORY OF THE WATCH CAME OUT.
MR DUNDAS WOULD NOT REMEMBER ABOUT
SCRATCHES IN WATCH IF HE COULD NOT EVEN
REMEMBER THE WATCH HE REPAIRED, BECAUSE OR
HIS DISCRIPTION OF WATCH IN FIRST PLACE.
THE SCRATCHES HE SAID DID NOT REVEAL
JACK THE RIPPER he was Right there
BECAUSE ALL IT SAID IS I AM JACK.
INITIALS AND J. MAYBRICK.
HOW WOULD ~~HE KNOW~~ WHAT THIS MEANT
15 MONTHS OR SO BEFORE THE STORY
ABOUT JAMES MAYBRICK CAME OUT.
AS FAR AS I AM CONCERND HIS SWORN
OATH IS COMPLETE BUNKUM A. Johnson.

CHAPTER 10

INK: A RECIPE FOR MADNESS AND DEATH

BY ROBERT E. ANDERSON

It is terrifying to contemplate the number of man-hours wasted in heated debate over the Maybrick Diary and Watch on the internet. I tremble to ruminate over how many hundreds of thousands of posts have been generated over the years, offering a tremendous amount of heat but very little light. All one has to do is check a few recent threads on JtRForums or Casebook to not only see the same points being argued about as fifteen years ago but that it's often the same people making them. In fact, I am getting a little twitchy from PTSD just re-reading my notes from a decade ago.

One of the great canards repeated ad nauseam over the past twenty-five years is that the Diary hasn't been properly tested, or for that matter not really examined at all except by carefully restricted people sympathetically predisposed for a favorable conclusion on the Diary's age. Nothing could be further from the truth.

In April of 1992 Michael Barrett, a scrap metal dealer from Liverpool, famously contacted Doreen Montgomery of the Rupert Crew Literary Agency and claimed he had the Diary of Jack the Ripper. Since that time numerous people have made claims and passed opinion on the diary but let us actually create a list of persons restricted to those that are professionally qualified and serious examiners, who have at least SEEN the actual Diary before giving an opinion:

Robert A. H. Smith	The British Museum
Brian Lake	Jarndyce Booksellers
Dr. David Baxendale	Forensic document examiner
Nick Eastaugh	Forensic document examiner The Tate
Keith Skinner	No introduction needed
Paul Begg	No introduction needed
Martin Fido	No introduction needed
Donald Rumbelow	No introduction needed
Anna Koren	Graphologist
Sue Iremonger	Document and handwriting examiner
Audrey Giles	Forensic document examiner The Sunday Times
Bill Fairweather	Book binding expert
The Rendell Team	Nickell, Kuranz, Owens and Rendell
Rod McNeil	Ion migration analyst
Dr. David Forshaw	Maudsley Psychiatric Hospital
Melvin Harris	(assuming he actually examined the Diary; it is not clear whether he did)
John Roberts	Professor of Paper Science UMIST
Alec Voller	Diamine chemist and ink expert
Peter Bower	Paper expert

In addition to this prestigious list of professionals there are also several well institutions that have had access to the diary for review and analysis including Analysis for Industry (AFI), Leeds University, Staffordshire University and, of course, Scotland Yard.

I am sparing the reader a discussion of the merits and qualifications of all of these examiners, researchers or institutions; a quick Google search on each of the names will reveal their role in the testing history of the Diary. I also heartily recommend Chris Jones' *Maybrick A to Z.* Bear in mind that these are just the Diary tests/examiners; there were three on the Maybrick Watch as well. As Robert Smith said to me:

"You still have a list of 25 or so qualified people/organizations, who actually examined the physical diary, and provided an opinion and /or a written report. None of them could remotely be classified as "pro-Diary", a ridiculous phrase to apply to independent examiners and scientific testing organizations."

Robert Smith, email correspondence 2012.

Mercifully, there is one significant area where progress has been made, at least in terms of the debate if not the facts. One thing less to argue about… And that has to do with the issue of what ink the Diarist actually used to write this infernal document. It is testimony to the irrationality of the Diary debate. While the ignorant were chanting, "Do the tests! Do all the tests!! Do all the tests now!!" the reality is that quite a few revealing tests had in fact been done. And it matters, because understanding the ink tests is in its own way as important as the provenance of the Diary. It was a matter of taking a step back from the madding crowd and looking at what tests had actually been done in the 1990s, by whom, and with what resources at hand. The answer was under our noses all along.

In 1992 Shirley Harrison commissioned Dr. David Baxendale to analyze the Diary ink using TLC. No, that is not tender loving care. It stands for thin layer chromatography and I will spare you a detailed discussion. It is essentially the technology police use when they analyze a drunken driver's breath test. It is crude and not that accurate and as you can see it does not separate out components cleanly or purely. Identification of components is not 100% accurate and you cannot quantify the amounts of each component.

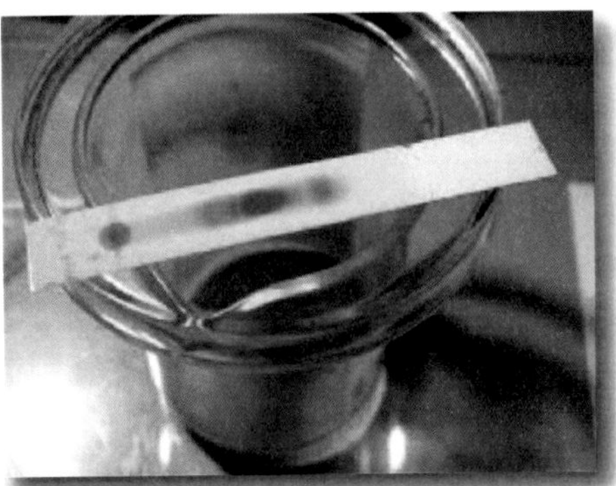

From https://commons.wikimedia.org/wiki/File:TLC_black_ink.jpg

Baxendale drew some wildly erroneous conclusions from his tests. He claimed there was no iron in the Diary ink, that it contained nigrosine dye which he asserted was not utilized before the First World War and that the ink was easily soluble from the paper. All three points are simply wrong. Of course, we are not sure what the proportions were of the solvents that he used to dissolve the ink. Leeds University, who have an excellent department dedicated to color chemistry, used methyl ethyl ketone and found the Diary ink did not dissolve readily from the paper. When some of his errors were pointed out to him Baxendale did modify his position in a third report to Shirley Harrison, stating on August 20th 1992, *"…if an ink known to have been applied to a document about a hundred years ago were found to have a similar solubility, then there would appear to be nothing in the chemical properties of the ink in the diary to preclude it being of a similar age."* (The Maybrick A to Z, Chris Jones, 2008). As for nigrosine dye, well it was actually patented in 1867 and was in fact used in inks in 1889! Unfortunately, Melvin Harris and the Sunday Times seized on Baxendale's earlier comments and used them in an attempt to discredit the age of the Diary ink and the publisher of Harrison's book, Robert Smith.

Photo of Robert Smith by Katja Nieder 2012

Dr. Nicholas Eastaugh is a well-respected expert in the technological study of paint and painting, and has authored a standard reference work in the field of pigments. Ms. Harrison reached out to him after reviewing Baxendale's problematic conclusions. Instead of TLC, Eastaugh analyzed the Diary ink and paper using Scanning Electron Microscopy/ Energy Dispersive X-Ray Spectroscopy (SEM/EDS). TLC would not work for analysis of sodium for example but SEM/EDX would be very accurate. There can be some issues with that latter technique revolving around the detections of elements with low atomic numbers, including Carbon (6), Nitrogen (7) and Oxygen (8). This is a concern if you are searching for Nigrosine which contains plenty of N

Structure of a major component of Nigrosine dye
From: https://commons.wikimedia.org/wiki/File:NigrosinChemDraw.png#filelinks

Eastaugh did not find it, nor evidence of any other synthetic dye.

Also, unlike other testers, he was tasked with examining the black powder stuck in the channel between Diary pages. He concluded that it was bone black based on the carbon and phosphorus he found. This is intriguing as bone black was used as a drying agent in the Victorian era. Like the writing sands we will discuss below, it raises serious questions because it is a telltale mark of authenticity; it's not something a modern forger is likely to have thought of.

On June 27th 1994, Michael Barrett made the "confession" that he had forged the Diary with assistance from is wife Anne. The ebbs and flows of Mr. Barrett's mind in those days are outside the remit of this essay. His tory was that he bought the Victorian-era scrapbook used for the Diary at an auction and acquired the ink at he Bluecoat Chambers art shop in Liverpool. He did not specify what brand of ink was purchased but a Liver- ool journalist by the name of Harold Brough contacted said shop and was informed that, while they did not ecall making the sale, if they had made such a sale, it would most likely have been a manuscript fountain pen nk, manufactured by Diamine, a local manufacturer of ink since 1864.

he issue of Diamine became the focus of a hotly-contested debate because Diamine contained chloroaceta- nide, a preservative. Chloroacetamide was not in widespread use circa 1888-89; Victorians typically utilized arbolic acid as a preservative.

he online debate over nigrosine and chloroacetamide, and the presence or absence thereof, became the be- ll-and-end-all of tens upon tens of thousands of posts, the vast majority of them from non-scientists. Many of hem read like science-based remarks, but it becomes clear on closer reading that the authors have copied and asted a variety of sources and typically make some alarming claims about the lack of equipment sensitivity or ppropriateness that are unfounded in the context of this sort of ink testing. Testing the Diary ink and paper is NOT rocket science! As a non-scientist, I suppose I must add myself to this long line of pundits. In my defense, am on the board of several biotech firms and have been able to get a great deal of guidance from their lab cientists and medical writers. Hopefully I am producing more light than heat.

t is important to state that my belief in the Diary's authenticity is not a matter of cherry-picking. It is not redicated on a selective battery of tests, or just those which I believe reveal favorable information. Many of he "anti-Diarist" tests were done at low cost using inappropriate lab equipment or with contaminated samples. To give just one example, AFI (Analysis for Industry, a two-person, husband and wife lab) tested the Diary ink n October 1994 using samples provided by author and broadcaster Melvin Harris and apparently obtained y him from a previous tester who had them left over from his own tests. I will spare the reader a recap of ny scintillating York 2012 talk on gas chromatography/electron scanning microscope analysis as I am told ecordings of it are currently used in operating theatres as a muscle relaxing agent. Suffice it to say the samples rovided to AFI had been stored in gelatin. It is extremely problematic for any lab to accept such samples for nalysis for the very simple reason that gelatin is incredibly permeable. Glass is standard for capsule storage. And said gelatin capsules had been stored in Melvin Harris's desk of all places. The possibilities for cross-con- amination of ink in the desk of an author are limitless. It is not an exaggeration to say that SEM/EDX spectra nalysis, if done correctly, could pick up the chemicals in a lab assistant's hair spray if she or he were to touch he sample with their bare hands. Here's a picture of Rendell team member Maureen Owens of The American Society of Questioned Document Examiners doing precisely that

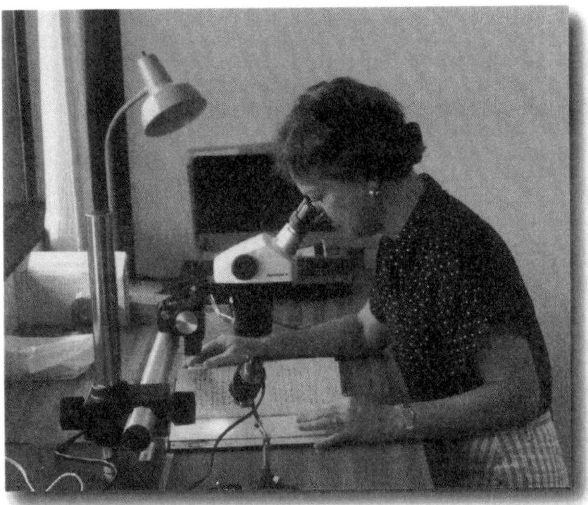

The American Society of Questioned Document Examiners.
Photo by Robert Smith. From http://www.asqde.org/about/presidents/owens.html URL.

But that is not what AFI used; they used a single column GC-FID (i.e. a gas chromatograph with one column and a flame ionization detector). The entire community of analytical chromatographers the world over would shudder over this.

Why? The answer in layman's terms is to compare the test to a horse race, which is a fair comparison because at the heart of it we are heating molecules and observing how fast they travel up a column. The AFI tests were hideously flawed. They generated signals but then had no device to determine what those signals were. Sort of like having a horse race, and posting the results... but all of the horses were the same color and size, had no numbers on them and were ridden by jockeys who were identical siblings wearing silks of the same design and pattern. So you know the fastest horse won but not who he was... same for place and show. And we would ask the horses' names and be met with a stare.

There is also the issue that AFI's equipment was contaminated; they used what a chemist would call a dirty blank. AFI's unclean blank (which can be deduced from the graphs they released) indicates their column was not flushed properly and that there was some residue from a previous analysis still remaining in their column. This is obviously going to distort results. If, for example, chloroacetamide was run through the column prior to the sample from the Diary, the results cannot be relied on in any fashion. It appears this was the case – they analyzed a concentration of chloroacetamide that was so high that even with a degree of flushing enough remained on the column to provide a trace reading when the Diary sample was run.

AFI found a trace of chloroacetamide, which was 5000 times less than the quantity required (3.28% of the dry ink) for the formula of Diamine Ink. Melvin Harris deceptively briefed AFI to report only on the presence of chloroacetamide, not the quantity. I mentioned this at York 2012 and Robert Smith details it in his new and highly recommended work, 25 Years of the Diary of Jack the Ripper: The True Facts on Mango Books.

In brief, the AFI results are worthless.

Let's move on to the tests run in 1994 by Leeds University Department of Colour Chemistry and Dyeing, which is considered to be one of the U.K.'s finest labs. Unlike AFI, they used the correct and much more accurate procedure of gas chromatography in conjunction with mass spectrometry. As Professor John Roberts, Professor of Paper Science, at UMIST Manchester said "This is a well-established technique for such work and should have been used [by AFI]. The identification is more or less worthless without it."

Gas Chromatography–Mass Spectrometry (GC–MS)

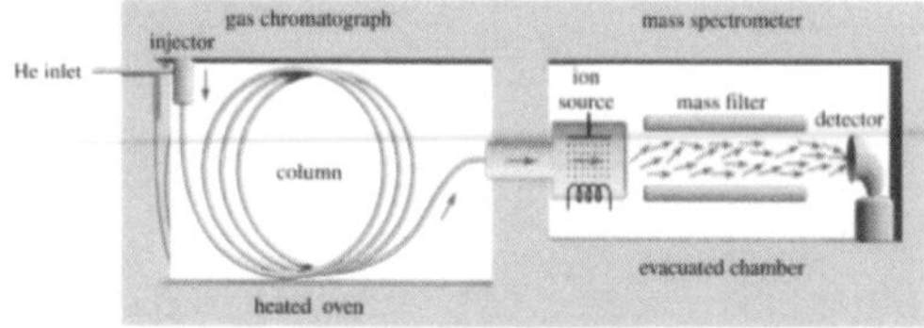

Copyright © 2010 Pearson Prentice Hall, Inc.

- The gas chromatograph column separates the mixture into its components.
- The mass spectrometer scans mass spectra of the components as they leave the column.

Organic Chemistry, 7th Edition L.G. Wade 2010

Returning to our horse race analogy, the gas chromatograph is the race course and the mass spectrometer is the photo finish that is able to identify exactly which horse finished first, displaying the results as a spectral graph.

Internet pundits had debated these ink analysis results for years, AFI versus Leeds, which was fascinating to me as no one had ever seen the actual Leeds results from their tests on the Diar

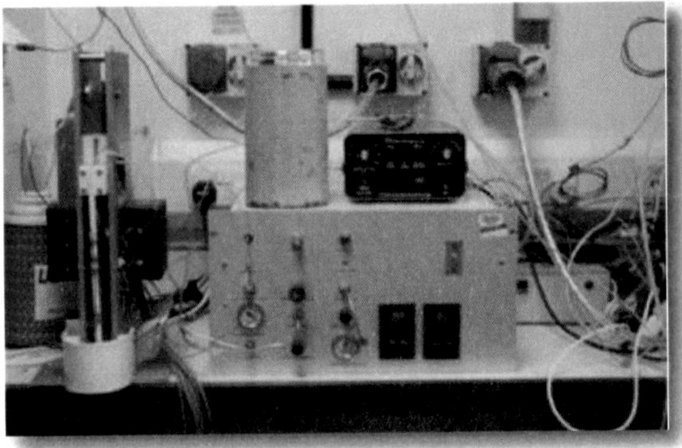

Gas Chromatography equipment, Leeds University

Crucially, the samples tested by Leeds were taken directly from the Diary using sterile equipment when the Diary was physically brought to the lab, which once again exposes as lies claims that the Diary was never released from Robert Smith's hands for in depth independent analysis. As you can see, this is not a home chemistry kit, and accordingly the Leeds tests did not come cheap. The Diary camp spent several multiples of what the "anti-Diarists" ever did for their testing. If one wants to cry out for proper, validated, independent cast your eyes at the following graph:

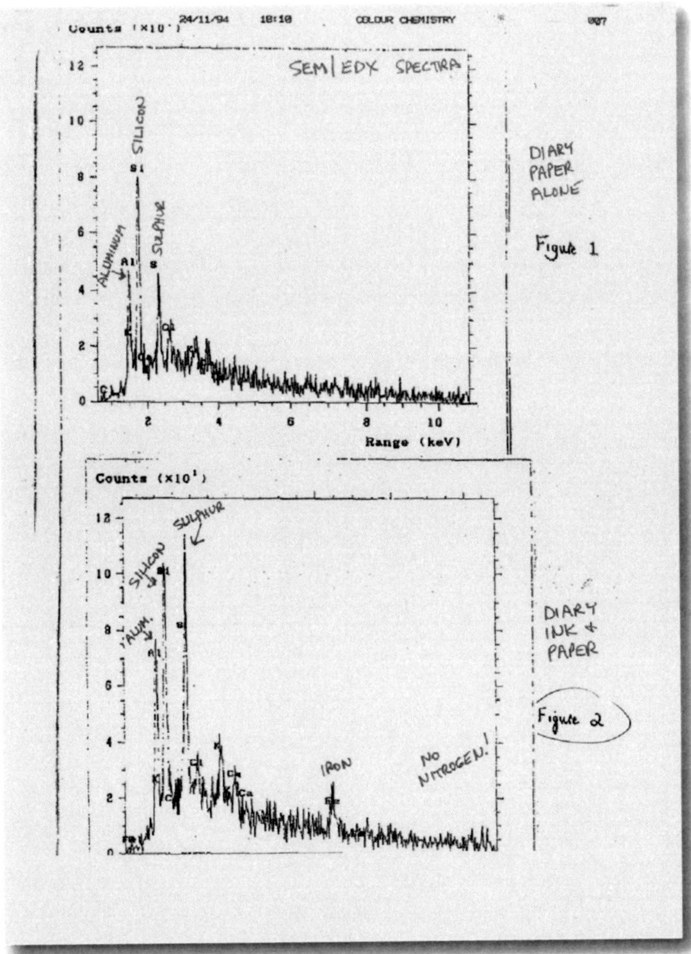

From https://www.chem.leeds.ac.uk/hirac-group/instrumentation/gas-chromatography.html URL.testing, ing graph.

In 2006, I spearheaded an effort to get a fresh look at the actual Leeds results, which you see above. The handwriting on the graphs is mine. Figure 1 is simply paper from the Diary; Figure 2 is the Diary ink plus paper. Chloroacetamide contains nitrogen (N), which makes up approximately 15% of its mass, and – unfortunately for the Diamine proponents – the Diary ink contains no notable traces of nitrogen. We can be sure of that as each element, be it iron, calcium, silicon, nitrogen or any other element you care to mention, appears at exactly the same place in the spectrum and there was no signal where nitrogen would have appeared if it had been present in the samples analyzed. Case closed – the only time these words will escape my lips in connection to the Ripper!

I was surprised at first to see aluminum (Al) in the spectra. However, Alum or aluminum sulfate has a long history in paper making as an adhesive to bind paper fibers (sizing). The Diary paper, which is indeed sized, is derived largely from wood pulp and cotton, the standard for paper from the Victorian era.

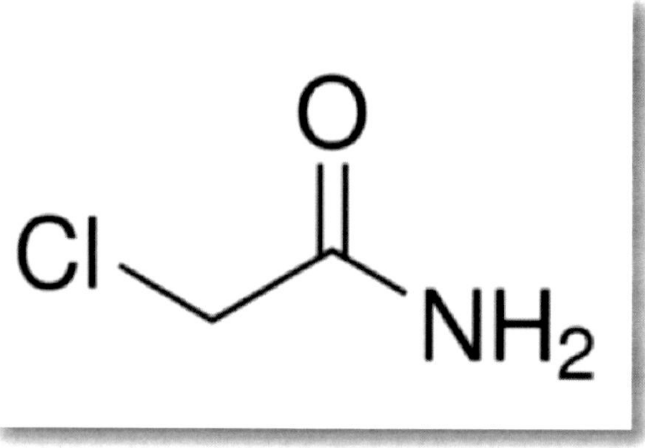

Chloroacetamide

The Diary ink does contain silicon (Si), iron (Fe) and dramatically higher levels of sulfur (S). The Si is intriguing because Victorian era "writing sand", used like blotting paper to soak up excess wet ink, contained hefty amounts of silicon (sand from Calais was once a favorite for this) and you will notice here how Si is in both the ink AND the paper. Writing sand came in particularly handy when the paper on which one was writing on was rough, which is the case with the Diary, as it was meant to be a scrapbook or memento book. (I understand that the pages had a divider to allow for the insertion of some bulkier items such as a theatre program or similar.) There are no circumstances under which I can envision Barrett utilizing writing sand!

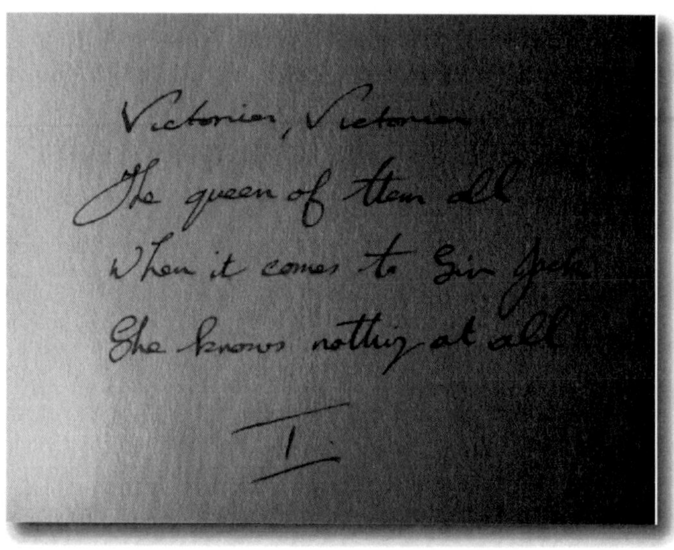

Chapter 10

So,we know what the Diary ink is not. But what is it??

I've read a lot about ink in the past few years, and one thing is very clear: ink manufacturers have guarded their ink formulas over the centuries like state secrets. They are even more secretive than Pepsi and Coke with their formulas. One can learn what went into a given ink, but things were (and are) constantly being tweaked. Proportions changed, secret ingredients added.... It has always been a competitive and innovative field. So the opportunity to be tripped up in analysis (or forgery for that matter) is endless.

I will remind the reader that the two most qualified ink analysts to have examined the Diary - Kurantz and Voller - are of one mind. (Kurantz, despite being a member of the Rendell team, repeated and endorsed Eastaugh's findings.) All have stated that there is nothing inconsistent with the ink being of the Victorian era. (You will rarely get a tester to state something definitively.... "not inconsistent" is pretty strong language for these guys.)

A brief history on ink is in order here. Very brief. The ancient Chinese used an ink consisting of carbon mixed with gum. Same for the ancient Egyptians. The good news is these inks do not fade, nor corrode the paper they are written on. The bad news is the ink essentially sits on the surface of the paper, and it is easy to scrape off or erase. The Greeks solved this by coming up with something that is a clear ancestor of the Diary ink. This type of ink is referred to as iron-gallotannate or iron gall ink. They took an iron salt (hydrated ferrous sulfite - remember this later when you wonder why the Diary ink contains so much sulfur) and tannin (gallotannic acid) and mixed them in water. They then threw in some gum for viscosity and binding. But if you just use this formula the ink is hard to see on the paper when you are writing, so they added carbon.

Now, as time goes by - and it varies radically with exact ink composition and storage conditions and paper quality - this iron gall ink turns from a dark grey to black. It really bites chemically into the paper. Document examiners are going to look at something like the Diary and try to determine the degree to which the ink has really combined with the paper, unlike the surface-lying Chinese and Egyptian ink types used for eons. Eastaugh and Leeds found the ink tightly bound with the Diary's paper. (In fairness, the Diary paper is quite thick and can be argued to be extra absorbent.).

Iron gall is corrosive to steel nibs, which were the norm by the 1850s, so manufacturers dialled down the corrosive elements and added dyes such as indigo. This produced a so called "blue black" ink and is the type of ink mentioned at the end of the Leeds report. The ink is blueish when it first hits the paper and turns black over time as the ink is oxidized, the rate of this happening depending on many factors, none of which could be predicted with certainly by a forger. Once oxidized the color is permanent and cannot be reversed, just as one cannot reverse the rusting of iron! Blue black ink was the manuscript standard for quite awhile.

This is almost certainly what you are looking at. A blue black iron gall ink, certainly commonplace in the Victorian era which of course does not prove it is Victorian. It just means the Diarist didn't bungle this aspect of the creation of the document, despite all you have read over the years. Recreation of old inks is not an impossible task but outside of a strict laboratory environment the avoidance of any modern contaminants is difficult, especially for amateurs not well versed in scientific protocols. Reconstitution of an old dried ink into utilizable writing ink is almost unheard of – if one could even purchase such an item, as postulated by Melvin Harris. I know – I tried to buy them in London for over a decade. Harris' erroneous ink dissertations still reside on the Casebook.org site. The A-Z refers to them as containing "much useful data". Well, they also contain outrageous and libelous assertions based on erroneous data from methodologically flawed tests. And as an aside, nigrosine ink was first produced commercially in 1867, so the comments of Baxendale and Harris are risible. Its presence would not be a knockout blow by any means. However, as David Carvalho says in Forty Centuries of Ink, "Nigrosine, one of the best known of [dyes], is much used as a cheap "black" ink, but as it is blue black and never becomes black, it really belongs to the family of "colored" writing inks. They possess an undeserved popularity for they flow freely from the pen which they do not corrode, nor do they thicken or spoil in the inkwell; they are however very "fugitive" in character and should not be employed for record, legal, monetary or other documentary purposes. The indigo and Prussian blue inks are well known, the former under certain conditions a very permanent ink, the latter soon disintegrating." A nigrosine based ink would not have resulted in the Diary we see today. Ironically, a nigrosine ink like Diamine WOULD have resulted in a blueish hue.

One is looking at a document written with a steel nib dip pen, which leaves a line that varies from dark to light as the ink on the nib runs out, and then becomes dark again as the writer redips the nib. An interesting element, at least to my eyes, is the fact that the Diarist used iron gall in the first place. It was more of a business ink. When laid down on paper, nigrosine ink offers a nearly black color (actually a very dark lilac that does not change or oxidize over time, although it may dim through exposure to light). It flows freely and does not corrode the pen. However, it never does reach the same deep black shade of a good iron nutgall ink and has the major disadvantage in being easily affected by wetting. Ink eradicators also easily affect it. Thus, it never achieved the popularity among businesses that it did among private citizens.

Ink Type	Business	Personal
Nutgall	83%	30%
Logwood	10%	45%
Nigrosine	7%	25%
Total	100%	100%

The Topic Is Ink Copyright ©Calvet Hahn 1981 From http://www.nystamp.org/postal-history-articles/the-topic-is-ink

I confess to having gotten a bit of a chill down my spine when I first realized the Diarist might have used a guard book kept in Sir Jim's office and the same business ink Maybrick himself might have used, just for jolly. Wouldn't you?

Now one of the characteristics of this iron gall ink is some degree of irregular fading: experts are uniform in stating this cannot be faked. Fading in this sense means that words right next to another – or one line versus another nearby – have rather different shades. It's not uniform, which something like artificial baking or a heat lamp would produce. Baking, by the way, can produce cracks in the ink like alligator skin. There are no signs of such anywhere in the Diary.

Alec Voller of Diamine Ink said: "The fading is typical of the way ink fades in documents of this era; the fading is uneven and its unevenness does not correspond with when the pen was dipped into the ink. Some places where the ink is quite heavy from a freshly dipped pen have faded noticeably, whereas other areas where the ink was running out have not faded at all." There is also the issue as we have said that blue-black ink takes a couple of years to turn black. In my humble opinion, it was Leeds' remark that the Diary ink might be "a blue black ink of the iron-gallotannate type, so pure that at first the solution was at first colorless yet turned black on oxidation" is what created the "found memory" that the ink was indeed blue when first viewed in 1992. Martin [Fido] felt that this was wrong and that he found that the ink in the 'diary' when he was first shown it was "too blue." He then said that it was too consistently blue throughout. He also added that he would have expected to see an ink type in a purportedly old document to be black turning brown, or blue with a coppery sheen on it. What Martin maintained he saw when he first encountered the 'diary' was clear blue going right through the text that was faded, but, Martin told me, this could be done by adding water to the ink as the late Melvin Harris had earlier suggested. (Adrian Morris, "Blue is the Color", Journal of the Whitechapel Society, August 2010)

Water would have given the ink a uniform thinness that the high-resolution scans in Robert Smith's new book show does not exist. In fact, far from it. I should also quote Martin Fido's somewhat more moderate comments on his own annotated copy of the 1994 Leeds Report - "Doesn't this bear on the feeling some of us had that the Diary ink looked too blue for its purported age?"

So, if Martin Fido is correct that the ink was bluish when he first saw it mid-1993, it means the Diary ink would have finished "turning" only in 1994 ... yet Voller clearly saw what was to his eyes an aged ink in 1995. Ink that was faded and bronzed in a few spots. And, of course, Baxendale, no friend of the Diary, described it as "dark grey" in 1992.

Here are three screen grabs from Martin Howell and Paul Feldman's excellent 1993 documentary The Diary of Jack the Ripper: Beyond Reasonable Doubt? The first is of Martin Fido examining the Diary, and the other two indicate the ink color as displayed in the film. I would affectionately ask my good friend and colleague Martin the old Groucho Marx question: "Who you gonna believe - me or your lying eyes?"

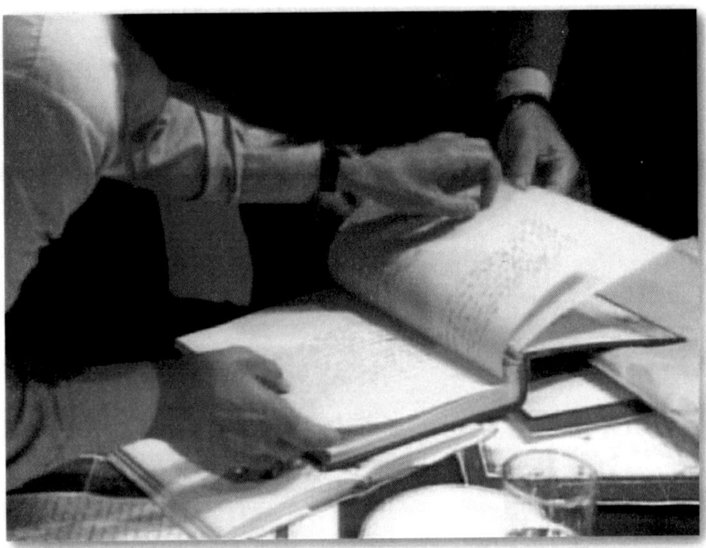

Screen grab from The Diary of Jack the Ripper: Beyond Reasonable Doubt
Copyright© Image Entertainment Inc. 1993

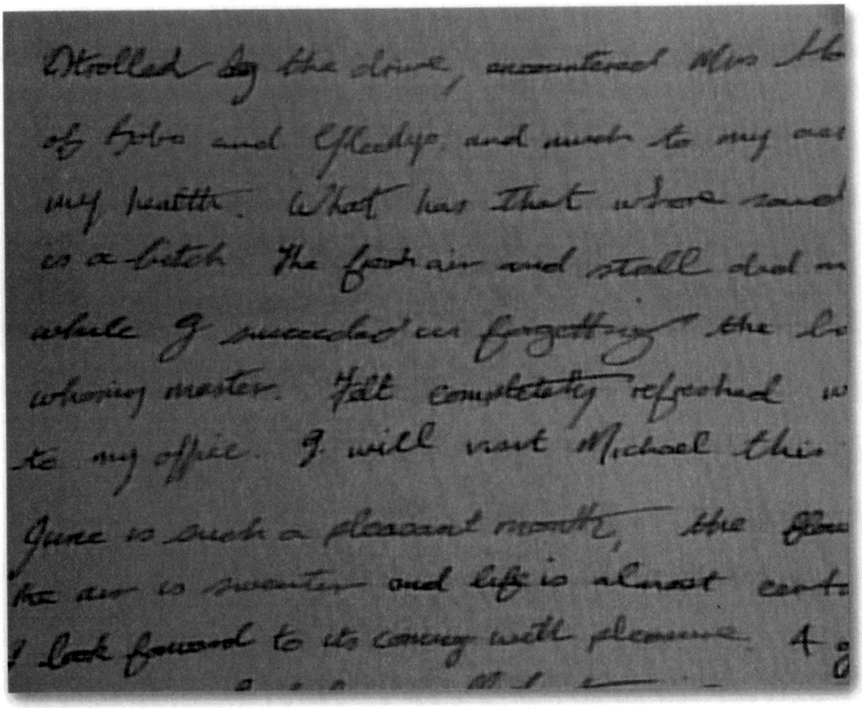

Strolled by the drive, encountered Mrs H
of Bobo and Gladys, and much to my
my health. What has that whore said
is a bitch. The fresh air and stroll did m
while I succeeded in forgetting the
whoring master. Felt completely refreshed
to my office. I will visit Michael this
June is such a pleasant month, the flow
the air is sweeter and life is almost cert
I look forward to its coming with pleasure.

Screen grab from The Diary of Jack the Ripper: Beyond Reasonable Doubt
Copyright© Image Entertainment Inc. 1993

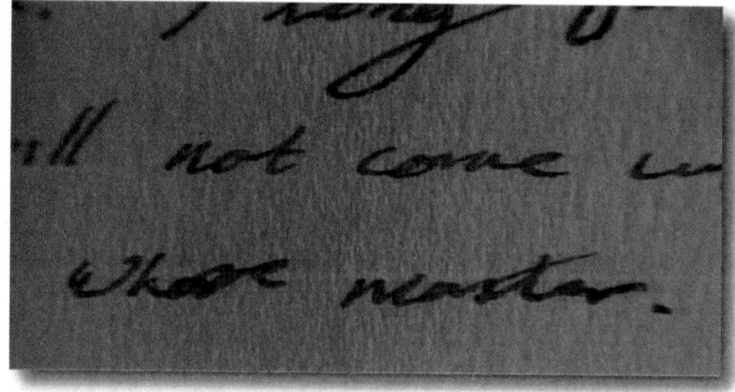

Screen grab from The Diary of Jack the Ripper: Beyond Reasonable Doubt
Copyright© Image Entertainment Inc. 1993

Author and Martin Fido at York Jack the Ripper Conference 2012

One last comment regarding bronzing or the "coppery sheen" mentioned above. If you were fortunate enough to examine the Diary at York 2012, you might have noticed a bit of it in the ink in two or three spots if you held the Diary to the light in the right angle. It is considered impossible to fake irregular bronzing. The subject could easily be its own essay, but I will just leave you with a lengthy quote from Voller by way of Shirley Harrison: "At this point Mr. Voller took the Diary to the window. "This is as I thought… it's barely visible… in one or two places there is some very slight bronzing …tilted to the light it can just be seen…'the children they distract me so I ripped OPEN'… the bronzing is in the last word… There is some more visible on the words' building up'. This tells me that it is genuinely old… This bronzing effect is a chemical process which is not fully understood… 'If you made up the ink in the way it is supposed to have been made up (as a modern forgery) it simply wouldn't have faded to the extent that parts of the Diary have faded… To create this document as a modern fake you would have to start with a person of at least my experience of ink…" (Harrison The Diary of Jack the Ripper: The Chilling Confessions of James Maybrick 1993)

Thanks for reading this far!! I would like to thank my colleagues at Team Syphilis for their massive help over the years, and of course Robert Smith the owner of the Diary for his gracious assistance over the many years as we grope for the truth, and try to avoid being groped by anyone in return. Special thanks and love are due to my colleagues Mank Hughes, Paul Begg, Katja Nieder, Livia Trivia, Dave Stokes, Robert Smith and Mark Ripper for their sharp editing pens and advice!

I hope you enjoyed reading this article, and that any old notions that Mike Barrett forged the Diary, or that the Diary has not been submitted for proper testing, have been dismissed and that you have instead some new perspectives on who the Diarist might have been, with his bone black, writing sand, and iron nut gall business ink.

CHAPTER 11

WHAT IS NOT WHAT IN THE 'MAYBRICK DIARY'

BY PROFESSOR DAVID CANTER

'The Diary of Jack the Ripper' has passed into legend as either a curious, historically accurate hoax or "The Chilling Confessions of James Maybrick", as Shirley Harrison subtitled her book about the document. But whilst the sequestered jury has its knock-about debate over which of these two possibilities to go for there are plenty of other aspects of the document that should be brought into public view. My claim is that there are many things that the document is not. Until we recognise what it is not, the discussion of what it is remains rather arid.

Firstly, there is a simple framework that describes the possibilities of authorship, that I will encapsulate in a technical format widely used in the social sciences.

The Document was written by:

Authorship		Murderer
A1. James Maybrick		M1. Jack the Ripper
	who was	
A.2 Someone who is not James who knew him (and wanted to indicate it was him)		M2. Not Jack the Ripper
A3 Someone who is not James and selected him for historical reasons		

This gives six possibilities of who wrote it:
A1M1: James who was Jack the Ripper
A1M2: James who was not Jack the Ripper
A2M1: Someone other than James who was Jack the Ripper
A2M2: Someone other than James who was not Jack the Ripper
A3M1: Someone who is not James who knew him and was Jack the Ripper
A3M2: Someone who is not James who knew him and was not Jack the Ripper

All except A1M1 are fraudulent options but with very different psychological, and indeed investigative, implications. I think, though, that all the possibilities that have been offered as claims for the document's authorship fall into one of these six options. Filtering out the most likely requires careful consideration of the document. I'm putting to one side questions of provenance in this discussion, for although accounts of brown paper parcels passed surreptitiously in Liverpool pubs, or passers-by picking up curious packages from builder's skips and the like, would carry some weight in evaluating the document, they could only ever provide circumstantial evidence about its origins and about authorship, that would need corroboration from other sources. For example, even if the document could be traced to where James Maybrick lived, Battlecrease House, this would not totally rule out A2M1, A2M2 and both the A3's.

There are also, of course the more conventional 'forensic' tests of historical authenticity, such as paper, ink, vocabulary and direct references to known facts. If the document continues to pass such tests, as Shirley claimed, this could help dismiss the A3s, in effect that it is a recent forgery, but not any of the other four possibilities. The document itself has to be examined for any further insights. But before I turn to the document itself I'd like to consider why it was welcomed with such sceptical outrage when it was first published.

Why the Diary is suspected of being fraudulent

One simple reason is the question already explored 'Why would a genuine JtR write such a document?' It seems remarkably dangerous for a serial killer to keep a log that indicates so clearly his murderous activities. It makes more basic sense to see it as either a hoax (A3) or a deliberate attempt to frame poor old Mr Maybrick (A2). But this raises further questions.

If it is a latter-day hoax (A3) why pick on James? What was there in the historical record that caused the hoaxer to think of an undistinguished cotton merchant who lived 200 miles from London's Whitechapel as the person to claim as JtR? The level of sophistication required for such a nuanced scam is remarkable. Surely someone so clever would want the world to know of his (most crimes are committed by men) skill. He would either have come forward or have left some clues somewhere. I know the person who presented the document for publication, Mike Barrett, claimed to have forged the document, but when I asked him and some students to forge some more, an American student did a rather better job of it. Also Mike, may he rest in peace, never gave any convincing explanation of why he would set about such an onerous task.

If the M2 hypotheses are correct why would someone who knew James want to point the finger at him? Even more importantly, why do that in such a way that the document might never be found or if found it could be a century or more after Maybrick's death? Of course, we should never forget we are dealing with Liverpool here, a tribal society, replete with vendetta's. I mention this as a born and bred Scouser, for whom, in my youth, the transfer of a football player from Liverpool to Everton was regarded as a heinous treason.

The *'Hitler Diaries'*

Another reason why the document was suspect from the moment it came into public view was the unfortunate timing that The Times and other major publications had their fingers burned over the purported 'Hitler Diaries' less than a decade before the Diary came to public attention. In a wonderful book detailing this fiasco Charles Hamilton revealed just how bizarre was the belief that those documents were genuine. His account also makes clear how different that hoax was from the Diary.

Gerd Heidemann Posing with the Hitler Diaries © copyright http-//hoaxes.org/archive/permalink/the_hitler_diaries.jpg

There was a strong, right wing political commitment by Stern magazine to whom they were presented, to believe in the claim that the writings were the genuine outpouring of Der Führer. Initially, also, the documents were not directly scrutinised by the experts who were asked to authenticate them. Instead a media storm blew up with many publications desperately wanting to cash in on the 'discovery'. Those who had the documents did not even have the knowledge of Gothic script that would have told them immediately that they were fraudulent. The writing used up-to-date orthography rather than the more archaic from that Hitler would have used. The fraudster apparently did not know the script I learned at school!

The scam was a thoroughly commercial one with the fraudster being encouraged through a middleman to keep producing 'diaries' after the first one was devoured so rapaciously by the German media. It was only when the documents became open to scholarly scrutiny that the fraudulent nature became apparent. But this embarrassment for Stern, The Sunday Times and other internationally significant publications, became part of media folklore so the emergence of the Diary a few years later was greeted with a collective 'Oh no not another one! Pull the other leg….'

I've always maintained that against this sceptical background, and the curious narrative that accompanied its emergence (gifts from people now dead, packages handed over like contraband in dodgy Liverpool pubs) the Diary was not given a fair chance. I insist that a document of such potential significance should have been the basis of a well-funded forensic, historical project. Not a biographer seeking opinions from whoever would offer them. Not a small-scale publisher keeping the physical object under lock and key away from scientific eyes. As Shirley makes clear in her vivid presentation of the Diary the 'experts' who offered opinions did not agree, and in some cases were clearly not really the experts they were presented as. These problems were further aggravated by passionate advocates of the genuineness of the Diary, such as Paul Feldman, trying to bulldoze its acceptance in the face of initial reasonable doubt.

The really curious consequence of this situation is that a document of such potential significance has never been the basis of any academic publications that I know of. This does mean there has been little, carefully scrutinised scholarship exposed for critical analysis in learned journals. An omission that I am working in redressing. This must, in part, be based on a careful consideration of what the document is.

What the Diary of Jack the Ripper is Not

The document is not a diary in any conventional sense. There are no dates. There are only a few accounts of what has taken place. It is more about what the author was feeling or thinking. To take just one example, more or less at random, in what Shirley labels as section 253 "The gentle man with gentle thoughts will strike again soon" is an indication of a plan as well as being a form of bravado. It is true there are moments of recall, as would be expected in a diary such as, "I was vexed with myself when I realised I had forgotten the chalk", but this is quickly moved on to the gory suggestion of eating a part of the victim's body the killer had taken. The accounts of what he has done are nearly always tempered with comments on his thoughts and records of what a 'clever fellow' he is. In addition, there are various sketches of doggerel. For example,

"One ring, two rings,
A farthing one and two
Then crossed out
Sir Jim will do true
Letter M its true"

This is the author communing with himself, using the document as a way of martialling and recording his thoughts. Most of it is not a confession in any strong sense, but rather a vehicle for him to enjoy what he has achieved and record his plan for his next 'escapade'. The dominant mood is one of anger and self-congratulation, but above all to record his feelings of achievement, 'I have shown all that I mean business, the pleasure is far better than I imagined.'

There are elements of self-justification, as there would be in any mémoire, especially one that purports to be written by a serial killer. The reasons given are very narcissistic ones to begin with. The murderous acts are to deal with personal suffering "They will suffer just as I have", revenge and rage being given as excuses for what he is about to do. This is a recurring theme, "My desire for revenge is overwhelming". But this does change at the very end where the writer makes clear that the document is for posterity "so history do tell".

Whether he started out writing with this intention is not clear. The document curiously opens half way through a sentence. It does not have the form of a declaration of some confession. Indeed, the opening has all the quality of recording stream of thought. The chilling sentence 'They will suffer just as I". Is followed by the apparent non-sequitur of a domestic matter of hearing from his older brother. But this seems to be a thought triggered both by his impending trip to London and his recognition that at some point his children will need to be cared for.

In my book Mapping Murder I do discuss the subtlety of how the Diary is written with a view to the possibility that it was authored by a gifted hoaxer. Turning to the various possibilities. Besides the one prospect that it is genuine A1M1.

A1M2: James who was not Jack the Ripper

What would be reason for James Maybrick creating a fantasy document based on what was publicly known about JtR? Certainly, the personal details about letters from his brothers, his particular soft spot for Edwin his youngest brother and business partner, all indicate a very personal knowledge of James' family relationships. But why claim to be JtR?

A2M1: Someone other than James who was Jack the Ripper

A3M1: Someone who is not James who knew him and was Jack the Ripper

Both of these possibilities suggest that the fraudulent purpose the document was to push the blame for the murders onto someone else. Creating a detailed revenge narrative in such circumstances is very clever. Also, the clear declaration at the end as to the identity of the author would fit an intention to 'fit up' James. But would such a purpose require the document was found rather sooner than a century later? I suppose it could be some sort of 'insurance' if the true culprit was arrested on suspicion of being JtR.

A2M2: Someone other than James who was not Jack the Ripper

This becomes a particularly difficult hypothesis to defend. A great deal of research would be needed to develop a 'confession' with the sort of personal details that are in the document. The rather haphazard nature of the jottings indicates someone who knows how to weave a convincing personal narrative, without over egging the pudding. I would certainly have been proud to achieve that, but rapidly must add I would never have the patience to search out all the details necessary. Such an author would surely be proud of the achievement? Would that person not either have embedded within the document some hint of its actual authorship, or within the last twenty years since the volume emerged have stepped forward to claim credit and, indeed, copyright?

A3M2: Someone who is not James who knew him and was not Jack the Ripper

For me this is the most difficult suggestion to support. Why would you go to such trouble to point the finger poor old James, not someone there is any evidence was disliked? There must have been many other ways to get back at James if that was the desire. Unless the hoaxer was playing a very long game, he or possibly she, would have wanted the document to be known about very early on. The only person I can think of who might have wield such a vendetta is the much-abused Florence, but all the indications are she went out of her way to help James when he was ill. There is also no indication that a) she was much of a novelist, or b) she ever admitted that she knew her husband was JtR.

With reference to A1M1, if genuine why would a serial killer keep such a journal? That takes us back to looking closely at what is actually written.

What the Diary Tells us about its author

There are some memoires, and even autobiographies of serial killers. They are invariably justifications, or even denials of any guilt. One or two are self-indulgent quasi-philosophical attempts to present the killer as some ort of mystic or revolutionary. There is one very nasty one that I know of, never published in Britain, that is a rather sadistic account of the killer's actions in support of how much he enjoyed what he did. The Diary relates a little to this, but focusses more on providing an unfolding account of the emotions and thought processes of the author, apparently in relation to the most horrific crimes.

Against this background it is surprising how little attention has been paid to what the document reveals about the author. This reminds me of cases I've worked on of abusive anonymous letters. People look for all sorts of linguistic clues, vocabulary or syntax, or even expect the handwriting to reveal character or even identity. But a careful reading of the letters invariably reveals what the specific point of it is and by that means, usually, the identity of the author. In one case I even told the organisation the name of the anonymous author. This was the only name mentioned in the letter, which was a clear attempt to exonerate him.

As I've said, the document is very curious. It is not a diary in any conventional sense. Even as a journal or log of activities, it is remarkably patchy. If we take it at face value, what is the point of it? I suggest it reveals a number of purposes the author might have for writing it. These are the overt reasons, rather than any subterfuge that may be involved if it is a hoax.

1. It is to help the author steal himself for what he plans to do.
2. His personal justifications for his actions are recorded in support of his plans.
3. As noted he vents his anger on the page, apparently unable to do it face to face.
4. As JtR's notoriety increases the author records his achievements and failures.
5. His 'cleverness' is noted a few times as if to bolster his self-esteem.
6. Eventually he realises the document has some historical value and decides to store it for posterity.

The document shows a man of some intelligence. Quite able to express his emotions, which are extremely volatile. The regularity and frequency with which the journal is kept indicates someone who is probably known to be hard-working and reliable. Yet, it reveals a lack of believing in his own self-worth by the frequent references to his murderous achievements and his cleverness.

The document is in some ways remarkably middle-class. The only word that could be considered unacceptable in civil discourse is 'whore'. There is no swearing as such, or extended tirade. Whenever an outburst occurs on the page the writing quickly moves on to some more anodyne comments. In this regard it is noteworthy that the author mentions more than once that he is a gentleman. He even indulges in the sort of word games that he apparently enjoys by indicating that he is known to be a gentle man.

"So, History Do tell".

Taking all these considerations together. The Diary is certainly a remarkable document. It does not deserve being kicked into touch as many have tried to do with it. I come back to what I said some years ago. James Maybrick needs a very good alibi.